SUPER CRAFTY

OVER 75 AMAZING HOW-TO PROJECTS

SUSAN BEAL, TORIE NGUYEN, RACHEL O'ROURKE & CATHY PITTERS

SASQUATCH BOOKS
SEATTLE

Printed in Singapore by Star Standard Industries Pte Ltd.
Published by Sasquatch Books
Distributed by Publishers Group West
10 09 08 07 06 05   6 5 4 3 2 1

Cover and interior photographs: Morning Craft
Cover and interior illustrations: Ryan Berkley
Cover and interior design: Stewart A. Williams

ISBN: 1-57061-450-4

Library of Congress Cataloging-in-Publication Data is available.

Sasquatch Books
119 South Main Street, Suite 400
Seattle, WA 98104
(206) 467-4300
www.sasquatchbooks.com
custserv@sasquatchbooks.com

CONTENTS

GROUP ACKNOWLEDGMENTS

Thanks so much to Nedra Rezinas for all her help and hard work, to Paul and Nancy Dickson for their invaluable help with publishing details, and to Sam O'Rourke and Kohel Haver for their legal advice and assistance. Thanks to Ryan Berkley for his amazing illustrations that truly brought us to life as superheroes, to JD Hooge and Betsy Walton for their gorgeous photography, and to Betsy Greer for her contributions. Thanks so much to Heidi Lenze, Dana Youlin, Karen Parkin, Tanja Alger, and everyone at Sasquatch, too!

Thanks to Archie McPhee and Cupcake Royale for adding that little extra something to our Seattle trips, to Stumptown Coffee for the buzz to meet our deadlines, to the Goodwill Bins for all the spectacular junk and supplies, to Greta and Cutty for being perfect doggie models, to Jo-Ann Fabrics for always asking us what we were making (even when the answer was "Pasties!"), to Trader Joe's for the cheap wine and great snacks, and to the city of Portland, Oregon, a haven for crafty girls like us.

Last, a very special thanks to our dear departed Rosie the bulldog for her beautiful book photographs.

INDIVIDUAL ACKNOWLEDGMENTS

SUSAN

First, I have to thank my wonderful husband, Andrew, for supporting me in all my freelance and crafty endeavors, even when they take over our entire house. This time he had to put up with debris from fifteen or twenty craft projects in progress as well as piles of Super Crafty chapter pages everywhere. Thank you for bringing me take-out, for reading everything I wrote, for always offering helpful suggestions, and for taking me on such a blissful vacation after the book was finally done.

A million thanks to my family, too: to my super-supportive mom, who loves to wear susanstars jewelry and tell all of her friends about PDX Super Crafty; to my brother David and his partner Dawn, who are always excited to hear about what I'm up to, and my adorable nephew Jules, who co-stars with me on my website; and to my aunts, Susan and Alice, my cousin Jamie, my uncles, Roy and Paxton, and my grandfather, Add, for all their support, past and present. Thanks to Paul and Nancy for widening the path for me, and for all their help along the way. Last, I want to especially thank my dad, who spent hours drawing with me when I was a little girl, and my crafty grandmothers—my Mee Mee, who cheerfully let me make such a mess of her kitchen while I was learning to bake, and my

Grandmama, who sewed me such beautiful sundresses, doll clothes, and ornaments.

Thanks to my favorite superheroes, Cathy, Rachel, and Torie—it was so much fun gluing and appliquéing with you, girls! Thanks to Fiona for teaching me how to sew in the first place, and for all of her helpful advice and encouragement; to Diane Gilleland for her creative contributions and for bringing Portland Church of Craft into my life; and to the craftistas of **www.getcrafty.com** for their suggestions! Thanks to my lovely crafty friends around the country, who inspire me every day; to all the amazing crafters and creative businesswomen who help me keep my head above water; and to my marvelous editors, especially Jean Railla, Debbie Stoller, and Tsia Carson.

TORIE

I feel so grateful to have such an amazing family. Thank you, Quentin, for your love, guidance, and encouragement in my crafting and in life . . . and for keeping me fed and sane and not divorcing me during six crazy months of late nights, long meetings, constant crafting, and a lot of shush-ing. A huge thank you to my parents for being so supportive and wonderful: to my mom for encouraging me to make things and to my dad for teaching me to make good decisions; and to Duwayne and Paige for being the best stepparents ever. Thank you to my sister, Taylor, for her beautiful artistic inspiration,

and to my brother, Jordan, for his unending positive energy. Endless love and thanks to my grandparents: my gramps, Ovid, for believing in me, and my grammy, Virginia, for her timeless sense of style; Grandma Olive, for many fond memories of holiday card-making and for showing me what it means to have inner strength; and Grandpa Dan for always encouraging my artistic interests. Thank you to Aunt Sheila for every amazing thing you've made for me, and also to Aggie and Sharon because you're extra special.

Where would I be without my friends and my pets? Thank you to Susan, Rachel, and Cathy, for being constant sources of inspiration and laughter. Thank you, Catherine and Erica, for being the best "roomies" ever and for always being able to pick up where we left off. Thanks, Meghan, for all of the fun craft nights and listening to my endless rambling, and to Tina for keeping in touch all these years. To Diane and the Portland Church of Craft for teaching me new things; Anjali, Brandi, and the ladies of The Switchboards for the business advice and inspiration. Thank you everyone at Chevalier Advertising and Choi's Martial Arts for all that you've taught me. And, finally, thank you to Kitty and Annie for being the sweetest snugglemuffins.

RACHEL

A million thanks to Danny, who is an amazing life partner. Danny, thanks for cooking for me, for always making sure there is wine in the house, for being patient when our house turned into a craft obstacle course, for always believing that I can do anything when I am in doubt, for your brilliant, creative ideas, and for always being there to pick me up when I take a tumble in life. Another million thanks to my mother and father, who always walk with me along my life path with open hearts, who are always amazed by all my creative endeavors, and who always offer outstretched hands for support, and wisdom that will live on for generations.

To my brother and his partner Julie, who always embrace my kooky ideas, who support me beyond my wildest dreams, and who never let me forget to laugh at myself. To my grandmother, who passed on to me her spitfire nature, the "Goodman Hips," and the determination to never give up. Thanks to my grandfather, who instilled in me his love of Stetson cowboy hats and photography. To Adeline, who taught me how to dissect owl pellets, and to Bruce, who let me eat the funny papers and told me I didn't have to listen to my parents at the Beach House.

To all my friends, who in some way play a part in this book by generously sharing their ideas, creativity, and passion and their desire to leave the world a better place. Thanks to everyone at Kartini for giving me a home at work, for nurturing the artist in me, and for always wearing Loo Loo. A special thanks to my crafty soul sisters: Cathy, for chang-

ing my life after my first trip to the Bins; Susan, for saving my life from fashion show hell by introducing me to the whole wide world of cool crafty girls; and Torie, for her unconditional kindness and wisdom beyond her years.

Last but not least, thanks to the dogs in my life. Thanks to Cutty for his regal nature and Snoop Dogg top hat. A very special thanks to Greta and Rosie, best friends and bulldogs, for looking smashing in all the dog attire!

CATHY

Thanks to my husband, Greg, for his unconditional support of my creative endeavors and for letting me turn our basement into a flamingo-pink crafty wonderland. He took on double the parental duties when I was drowning in craft projects, he supported me when I quit my crappy job to do what I loved to do, and he is so incredibly tolerant of the constant flow of junk into our house. Thanks to my amazing son, Levi, who was so patient when I was working on this book and couldn't give him all my attention. He keeps me grounded and has taught me so much about art by showing it to me through his eyes. I especially want to thank my mom, to whom I dedicate this book. She taught me everything I know and is a true crafty queen. She is my role model as both a mother and an artist and is that one person who thinks everything I do is absolutely amazing, no matter what. Thanks to my sister

Caroline and my sweet niece Sydney, for moving their lives to Portland to be close to me. I love you guys!

Thanks to Rachel, Susan, and Torie for being the best partners in crime a girl could want! Thanks to my motherhood girl gang for all their encouraging words, for always listening to my rants, and for taking me out for drinks when I really needed it. Thanks to all the amazing friends that I have met in Portland who have helped make this my home. Thanks to the Pitters family for their love and support. Thanks to my dad for passing on the junk collector gene to me. Thanks to Elvis for the divine inspiration. Thanks to kitty queens Trixie and Jinx for being my girls. And lastly, a special thanks to the incredible crafty ladies from my past whose constant presence inspires me—my grandmothers Elba and Cecelia, and my great-grandmother Cora.

INTRODUCTION

S*uper Crafty* started out when the four of us were drawn together by our mutual love for and fascination with crafting. We always wished for a craft book like this one—filled with cool ideas on how crafting can enhance your daily life, plenty of recycled and repurposed craft projects, and modern takes on everything from skirts to shrines—and when Sasquatch tracked us down, we couldn't wait to get started. Each of us is happiest when we are crafting up a storm, so once we started collaborating and inspiring one another, we came up with dozens of project ideas!

We hope that *Super Crafty* will inspire you to create your own unique crafts, too. We included plenty of variations for each project, so you can personalize everything you make, from wrist cuffs to tiaras. Visit our website at **www.pdxsupercrafty.com** for lots more ideas, resources, and craft projects—we'd love to hear from you, too.

Happy crafting!
Susan, Torie, Rachel, and Cathy

SUPER CRAFTY MANIFESTO

WHY HANDMADE?

RACHEL

Before I could form sentences, I created drawings, paintings, and paper-mache sculpture globs. I went through the stage, as most kids do, of drawing arms and legs directly jutting out from everyone's heads. These drawings ended up on several of my dad's neckties, thanks to my mom's craftiness with special iron-on paper. My dad wore these ties religiously to meetings, even once when he was interviewed on TV. Another really crafty way my mom transformed and celebrated artwork created by my brother and me was to make needlepoints based on our drawings. My brother's drawing of our family driving a train over the mountains was needlepointed and displayed alongside the original drawing in our family room. My mom also changed my life forever by introducing me to the world of shrink art. She knew about shrink art before it was actually packaged and sold. We used to go to the local grocery store where each week the butcher, who knew my mother by name, collected a stash of liver lid containers for us. My brother and I would carefully draw elaborate scenes on the lids with permanent markers and then gather in front of the oven to watch the lids shrink into beautiful small discs.

Thanks to my parents' constant affirmation of our creativity, my brother and I considered ourselves artists starting at a very early age. Using my hands to create imagery, to share windows into my imagination, has always seemed magical. When I was in elementary school, seeing my mom constantly using her hands to create everything from our bell-bottoms and macrame plant holders to needlepoints and lost-wax cast jewelry solidified the idea that crafting and art making are an integral part of everyday life. Today my mom knits amazing, wearable art pieces and reaffirms the idea that crafting and art making are lifelong joyful pursuits.

My father, who is a loyal and inquisitive art and craft appreciator, has also played a major role in my creative development. He shared his enthusiasm while allowing me to develop my voice as a young artist. One day while visiting my dad in his office, I drew a picture of a parade of cats going down the sidewalk, up a tree trunk, around the leaves of the top of the tree, down the other side of the trunk, and onto the other side of the sidewalk. I remember my dad saying to me, "I'm so glad you let the cats go up the tree and back down instead of making them go around the tree. This way they get to have a real adventure!"

Many young artists need creative collaborators. My younger brother was my drawing buddy and fellow storyteller. We created elaborate stories of adventure to describe our sometimes rather abstract drawings that always ended up in frames or plastered all over the refrigerator. Occasionally my brother also became my unintended craft victim. After my parents brought home a book on how to make mud pies using "supplies straight from your own backyard," my mom discovered, to her horror, that I was trying to feed my brother a fresh mud pie for dessert after our picnic lunch.

As I grew older, my parents and their friends continued to influence my creative development. I went to work for Sandra Shannonhouse and Robert Arneson, both incredible artists in their own right, as the studio clean-up girl. I witnessed the creation of ten-foot-high self-portrait clay busts and whimsical metal sculptures. I saw how artists use their life experiences to express deep feelings, how creativity can fuel life, and how art can help people maintain dignity as they die.

I went on to formally study art in college, and then one day found myself living on an artist's *kibbutz* in Israel. For two years I worked with refugee and immigrant children, who without artwork had no way of communicating their experiences with war. I started to learn how art could help children heal from unspeakable traumas. I met an amazing woman on the *kibbutz* who introduced herself as an "art therapist." Everything fell into place for me. I returned to the United States and to the School of the Art Institute of Chicago to study art therapy.

Studying and practicing art therapy has enabled me to transform my art and craft making from a highly reclusive, individualistic practice to a communal, community-based practice. Each day as I practice art therapy or collaborate with fellow artists or crafters, I learn something new about myself. I owe many thanks to my life teachers, who continue to help me grow as an art therapist/social activist/artist/crafter, and as a person: my partner Danny, who is a master sculptor, cook, and creative conversationalist; my mom, who continues to blow my mind with her amazing knit creations and with her passion for creating things from scratch; my dad, the philosopher and master storyteller who always seems amazed each time I bring home a new piece of art; my brother, who has surprised us all by becoming a photographer of nature and surfers; my grandmother, the keeper of family folklore; my clients, who courageously reveal their innermost thoughts in their artwork before my eyes during art therapy sessions; and my friends, many of whom are amazing crafters, artists, and social activists.

CATHY

Creating is so instinctual for me that I never really thought about where it comes from. It doesn't feel like something I choose to do; it is more something that I *have* to do to live. I can't function well if I am not creating.

I come from a long line of crafty women. One of my grandmothers was a whiz with a sewing machine, making her own clothes as a young girl in the 1930s and '40s. My other grandmother majored in home economics in college and did amazing things with Styrofoam balls and sequins. Then there's my mother. She taught me to sew before my feet even reached the pedal. She made matching outfits for my dolls and me. She brought me to craft fairs in the 1970s, where she would sell out of her beanbag frogs and horseshoe-nail necklaces. She encouraged me and my sister to make all of our gifts. One year we made candles out of melted crayons. Another year we painted faces onto rocks. My favorite, though, was the year we made ashtrays out of large clamshells. (Where did she come up with these ideas?) She taught me that giving a handmade gift meant more than buying something at the store. It wasn't until recently that I saw the direct line between what my mother taught me as a child and the crafty woman I am today. Thanks, Mom.

I am a mother now and I do all sorts of wacky craft projects with my son. He has his own table next to mine in the craft room. We hand-make Christmas gifts, and he even sells his clay sculptures alongside me at art fairs. He usually uses the money he earns to buy someone else's art. I am proudly continuing the tradition that I learned from my mother and that she learned from hers. When you make something by hand, you end up with far more than a candle or a shell ashtray; you gain an invaluable experience that will stay with you for a lifetime.

SUSAN

My first crafty memory is of the excitement of coloring a life-size outline of myself at age three. I had never drawn on such a big piece of paper, and the whole time that I had to lie still so I could be traced was agonizingly slow—I couldn't wait to start drawing! I loved to draw paper dolls, cats and dogs, trees, my house—anything and everything I could think of. My favorite thing as a child was a new box of sixty-four crayons with the little built-in sharpener on the side. I used to draw dozens of paper dolls with elaborate wardrobes, reducing the purple and pink crayons to dull little nubs.

Though I sewed felt doll clothes by hand and collected beautiful fabric when I was a little kid, I didn't learn to sew with a machine until I was twenty-five—my art classes all through school didn't leave time for home ec. I was too intimidated to try using a sewing machine until my best friend from high school came to visit me for a week and we made a dress from a vintage pattern! Next came exciting solo projects—curtains, an apron, pillows, and a messenger bag—and two months later, my crowning achievement: a Western-style dark brown corduroy jacket with snaps, which I made for my boyfriend as a surprise for his birthday. For me, getting an idea for a skirt, sewing it, and wearing it out the same night was like suddenly discovering a new superpower.

Sometimes I wish that I had taken home ec classes with my friends and gotten started ten years earlier—but part of what I love about sewing is that I learned, and started making things, because I wanted to, not for a grade. There's something really incredible about figuring a craft out by yourself, or learning from friends or family: All the mistakes and all the triumphs are yours, and you can be intuitive and creative on your own time.

Around the time I started stitching away (and started my little handmade business, too), I found an amazing crafts website, **www.getcrafty.com**, that rocked my world. Over the last four years, I've gotten millions of ideas; given and received advice on finishing projects; hosted Naked Lady Parties (see page 157); and traded craft supplies, handmade postcards, ornaments, and presents with other crafty girls. My pen pals across the country have turned into some of my closest friends, and though we live in the same city, I even met Torie through getcrafty!

Meeting for drinks and knitting, or coffee and collage, and just chatting with friends who love to create as much as I do feels like an amazing, modern

spin on the quilting bees of our great-grandmothers' era. When I start sewing and realize that three hours have passed in a flash, or create a new pendant that I can't wait to put on, I know how lucky I am to spend most of my life working on beautiful things—and writing about them!

TORIE

I've been crafting for as long as I can remember. My mom always encouraged me to make gifts and cards for my family for birthdays and holidays. We made all sorts of fun things together—from Christmas ornaments out of walnuts and pompons to Halloween costumes and frosted cookies. My dad is also quite crafty. He has created some amazing wood furniture that will be treasured in our family for generations to come.

I feel so fortunate to have creative parents who taught me the importance of craft through their actions and helped define the role that crafting plays in my life. A life without crafting would be very unsatisfying to me. Creating things with my hands is rewarding and relaxing. When I'm crafting I feel content: I can clear my mind of anything that happened during the day and just focus on what I'm making. Even though it's the process of crafting that I love the most, it is so satisfying to finish a project and look at it knowing I made it myself.

When I was younger, I had no interest in learning to sew. It wasn't until my twenty-fourth birthday that I asked for a sewing machine and the help of my mom and grandma to teach me some sewing basics. Now I love to sew and have a passion for fabric and textures, bright colors and bold patterns. I thrive on welding them together with a needle and thread to create decorative functional items, like handbags and small accessories. Sewing has opened up an entirely new creative outlet for me. I also love that through sewing, I feel like I'm carrying on a tradition. Though sewing was once considered "women's work," a new generation of crafters is doing a wonderful job of gaining respect and appreciation for crafts in general, especially those that were traditionally done by women. I'm thrilled to be a part of this generation and enjoy helping people see the importance of crafting.

One of the great things about crafting is that there are no rules. You get to take all of these pieces and parts and put them together however you like to make a new whole. There is no limit to the possibilities of things you can make—and objects you can use to make them. Inspiration is all around us.

Living in a time when almost everything is generic and mass-produced, buying and wearing handmade items allows people to express their individuality and own something unique. That's why it is crucial that we support artists and crafters who are pursuing their passions and sharing their creations. To me, a handmade item is so much more meaningful than something made by a machine: Someone put thought, time, and feelings into making it. I always try to give as many handmade gifts as I can. My friends and family really appreciate the thoughtfulness of a gift that was made especially for them, or of a unique gift that I picked out from another crafter with them in mind.

I will continue to craft for the rest of my life and hope to help others discover the joys and wonders of crafting too.

SOCIAL CRAFT ACTION

How can your crafting make a difference in creating social change in your community? What role does crafting play in activism?

Looking back a century, we realize that activist crafting is not a new concept. Jane Addams, a social worker and activist in the late 1800s and early 1900s, founded Chicago's Hull House, establishing art centers and crafting circles accessible to the poor and marginalized in society. Extending her social craft action a step further, Addams organized art exhibits featuring the work of new immigrants and the poor. The revolutionary ideas that art and craft belonged to the masses and that each person possesses an innate ability to be an artist drove this early movement. Jane Addams's community artwork helped solidify the principle that craft and art are central to our own humanity and should be accessible to all.

Creative people have also effected great social change in times of war or political repression throughout history by making protest art. Graphic images and themes in political artwork engage the viewer with powerful imagery, which inspires an emotional response and presents the viewer with an undeniable visual truth. Some of the most extraordinary protest art survives attempts of government censorship and continues to inspire generation after generation of artists to take action. Artists are far too creative to be silenced and have always been involved in political movements, from Picasso's *Guernica* to the painted art banners depicting the plight of the migrant farm workers in the 1970s to the giant puppets at the 1999 World Trade Organization (WTO) protests in Seattle.

Action is another crucial component of activism—the energy that brings messages to people can be as important as the messages themselves. The art and craft process brings people together and can inspire them to discover a common voice. People engaged in social craft action can confront societal injustice, challenge the status quo, and call for change. When people who share common concerns join for social craft action, the results are exciting and often life changing.

Innovative changes to American society like women's suffrage, the forty-hour work week, and the civil rights movement weren't pioneered by elected officials, but by steady and strong activism on a personal level. There are creative ways to volunteer your time every day of the year, as simple as adding your voice and energy to your community.

Torie teamed up with Betsy Greer of **www.craftivism.com** to bring you more ideas on using crafts to create a better world. Visit **www.pdxsupercrafty.com** to see what you can do!

We are excited to share some of our own experiences with social craft action, and we hope these stories will inspire you to take action in your community today!

RACHEL

Even those who have never encountered a gun are aware of the widespread presence of guns in our communities, witness news reports of gun-related crime, domestic murders, and high-profile shootings at schools, churches and other public places. The ever-present fear that someone we love might be killed or injured is another form of gun trauma."

—*From the Bell Campaign's website,*
www.bellcampaign.org

While working as an art therapist with war survivors and gang-involved youth in Chicago, I witnessed the physical and psychological aftermath of gun violence. Hearing story after story about how gun violence forever traumatized individuals, families, and communities, I was driven to take action.

Helping children and their families pick up the pieces following gun violence trauma inspired me to work on a larger level to effect change through the art process.

I decided to use my art and craft skills and art therapy training to launch a community social action project to raise awareness of gun violence. In 1999, I started the Paper People Project, an international arts installation with a simple concept: to invite people to create artwork in response to their ideas, feelings, and experiences related to gun violence. Participants use the same human form outline for their artwork, and each human form is linked together to create an installation. More than 4,000 Paper People artworks have been collected from across the United States, Israel, Canada, France, Germany, Korea, Bosnia, Somalia, and Mexico. The universal response to the Paper People Project speaks to the capacity of art to transcend language and cultural barriers, enabling people to join together against human injustice around the world.

The success of the Paper People Project confirms that people often respond to imagery on a much deeper level than numbers and statistics. Imagine walking into a gallery, a school, or a community center and facing 4,000 works of art, each created by a different person, but joined by a common theme. People of all ages created artwork to memorialize loved ones killed by guns, while at the same time depicting the physical and emotional aftermath of gun violence.

Of course, there is still more work to be done on the issue of gun violence. I recently became a member of the National Rifle Association (NRA) in response to the appalling continued lack of gun control and the 1992 Assault Weapons Ban's expiration in 2004. As a member of the NRA, I am working both inside and outside the corrupt system, using both the written word and images to enact change.

Visit **www.paperpeopleproject.org** for more information or to join the Paper People Project. Perhaps you'll be inspired to think about an issue that impacts your community—and then act on it with art to create a powerful public response!

CATHY

Recycling isn't just about sorting the glass and the plastic. It's about reusing the stuff that is already here rather than producing new stuff, or inventing a whole new use for something. It's about turning junk into art. One way that I use art for social change is to create one-of-a-kind pieces out of objects that I find at thrift stores, at estate sales, or even on the street. You don't need to spend a ton of money at the craft store to be creative. By using found objects, you're not only saving money, but you're also keeping garbage out of the landfill. You wouldn't believe the amazing supplies you can find secondhand—vintage buttons, feathers, sequins, metal glitter, fake fruit, sewing trims, scrap wood, boxes, maps. It's all out there if you only look.

I recently worked on an art installation with my friend and neighbor, Carye Bye. We were invited to participate in the St. Johns Window Project, an annual event in which artists from North Portland create and install art in the windows of businesses in the St. Johns neighborhood. Carye and I came up with the idea to collect found objects and trash from around North Portland and arrange them into a kind of mosaic. Our goal was for viewers to see one large image from far away, but upon closer inspection, notice the individual small pieces. We wanted to show that the ordinary trash discarded on the street could be reinvented to become something beautiful.

We spent the summer going on trash-finding bike rides and walks and found ourselves constantly looking down, always on the lookout for that perfect item to add to our collection. We carefully stuck to our rule that all items had to be found in our North Portland neighborhood. We would often lament about the cool item we saw in another part of town that we had to pass up. By the end of the summer, we had quite a collection of inspiring items: several pencils, plastic flowers, wrappers, bottle caps, cigarette lighters, playing cards, a watch face, a cocktail umbrella, a plastic grasshopper, a heart-shaped

barrette, a spoon, and a door hinge—all things that were either lost or discarded.

Over the course of two late nights, Carye and I assembled our found items into the stunning image of a holy saint. We called her "Our Lady of North Portland." Her face was a smashed paint can, her halo was a child's toy parachute, her robe was a jumble of blue objects, and her glowing heart was a valentine chocolate box found floating in the Willamette River. She was on display in downtown St. Johns for a month, and many viewers told us that it made them see garbage in a completely new way.

SUSAN

Like Cathy, I also try to reuse as much as I can, and I vote with my wallet—I don't spend my money at giant chain stores or on sweatshop-made clothes, unless it's absolutely necessary. Instead, I try to buy handmade and local, and I trade my own work for everything from haircuts to web design. Most of my favorite clothes that I didn't sew myself are vintage or swapped at Naked Lady Parties (NLPs). An NLP is a perfect way to get tons of new stuff without spending any money—find out how to host your own on page 157. I also try to walk or take public transit to run errands, I write letters to the editor about things that make me mad, and I go to the movies at independent theaters instead of huge megaplexes. Think about where your money and energy goes—small changes can really add up when you're saving the world from mass production!

I can't afford to donate much money to the causes I want to support, so I give my time or my handmade pieces instead. My small donations of handbags and jewelry to charity auctions have helped raise money for orphanages in Africa and medical research here in the United States. I also give a percentage of my handmade art sales to Oregon Food Bank and Planned Parenthood every year at holiday time. Organize your own benefit or contribute to one that's already going.

Whenever I have time to volunteer, I teach art at a downtown public school. Portland Public Schools cut art classes out of elementary and middle school curriculums a few years ago due to lack of funding. The budget for an entire semester's art class is $30, so we ask parents to donate art supplies—basically anything and everything, from old magazines to new boxes of crayons. Each week my kids choose what they want to make, and I figure out how the heck to do it with what's in the donation storeroom. It's so much fun chatting with the kids while we make marble magnets, collages, and cards, and last year I even stretched the budget to buy us pizza for our last class together.

I loved my art classes so much as a kid, I can't imagine going through school without the chance to be creative. If you have time to volunteer in a local school or organization I can't recommend it enough,

it is so rewarding and fun. See **www.pdxsupercrafty. com** for ways you can get started volunteering or doing your own activist crafting.

GLITTER THERAPY

What drove millions of women in the 1970s to make brown and orange macrame wall hangings and plant holders? Why do so many of us spend hours and hours latch-hooking rugs on a Saturday night?

Our culture constantly rediscovers what other cultures just accept as a necessity of life. Crafting, to make things by hand, is an innate human need. Why do many of us feel so much better when we are crafting? You missed your morning coffee, got into an email fight with your boyfriend, and came home to find a lovely accident left by your dog. Why does all of this become irrelevant as you knit with your new fluffy yarn? Crafting soothes the mind, keeps your hands and mind creatively activated, and can be a restorative force in your life.

Why is crafting so healing? Our personal experiences as crafters and as artists, and what we know about the field of art therapy, inform our belief that crafting is a nourishing experience for individuals, groups, and communities. Art therapy involves the creative process of making art to heal and enhance people's lives. Through creating and talking about art and the process of art making with an art therapist, one can increase self-awareness; cope with symptoms, stress, and traumatic experiences; enhance cognitive abilities; and enjoy the life-affirming pleasures of artistic creativity. How does making a shrine for a loved one who has died, or sewing yourself an A-line skirt, apply to the field of art therapy? We suggest that the process of crafting can play an important role in lifting one's mood, in developing daily rituals of self-care, in bringing people together to build community, in creating powerful symbols to deal with difficult life issues, and in feeding the creative spirit.

RACHEL

My experience teaching knitting to girls with eating disorders solidified the idea that crafting has the capacity to help heal the mind. Many of the teen girls I work with as an art therapist, in what I call my "other" life, suffer from intense, overwhelming negative thoughts about their bodies. One day I brought yarn and knitting needles to a girls' group at the outpatient clinic where I work. Once the girls got past the often horrendous process of learning how to cast on, they went to town. They became bionic knitters. They asked if they could knit during all their groups, during medical check-ups, and during school. Within days they knitted scarves, and then moved on to hats and afghans. Within weeks, two girls in the group decided to start selling their scarves to raise money

to buy knitting supplies for hospitalized girls so that they, too, could learn how to knit immediately. Why did knitting catch on like wildfire at the clinic? Knitting is repetitive and meditative and can help refocus the mind from feeling anxious to quietly contemplating colors of yarn, patterns, and future projects. Now knitting is sort of a rite of passage at the clinic, and out of the corner of my eye I often catch a glimpse of a girl in an exam room knitting away on a new scarf.

CATHY

I always remember playing with tiny things as a child. Whether it was my dollhouse furniture or my miniature stuffed animals, I'd spend hours arranging and rearranging these small items. I'm pretty much doing the same thing as an adult, only now it's my art. I create tiny dioramas using found photographs, boxes, and odd pieces. I am making little scenes from the past and preserving frozen black and white moments in strangers' lives. I'm not sure how to explain it, but creating these shrines gives me comfort in my present life and in my relationships from the past, and it keeps me sane and leveled.

Art is my therapy. When I'm going through a hard time or feeling stressed, I always turn to crafts. Somehow, working with my hands and methodically creating something from nothing makes the bad stuff go away and the comfort set in. It's so important to have something that gives you that feeling.

Art is also a way to express emotions in ways that might not otherwise be possible. I struggled for years to deal with the loss I felt when my dad passed away. I couldn't bear to look at his belongings or even pictures of him. For nearly eight years they sat at the back of the closet in a box marked "Dad." One day, while I was working on this book, I decided to create a shrine to him using some of those belongings. The process of creating that shrine was more valuable than any other therapy I could have tried. Handling the items and arranging them in a new way to create something positive was therapeutic and cleansing. You can see the shrine, entitled "LHZ," in the Healing Crafts chapter on page 109.

SUSAN

As a freelance writer and editor, I spend a lot of time on deadline and on the computer. Making something beautiful by hand feels like a mini-vacation from the modern world—an escape from emails and ringing cell phones.

Knitting and making collages are my two favorite ways to reconnect with my creative self in the middle of a day of proofreading or doing my horrifically complicated Schedule C taxes. After four years of knitting, I'm still what I would charitably call an advanced beginner (I pretty much make rectangles),

but no matter what I'm knitting, it is just magical watching my creation fly off my needles. Making collages and arranging my trinkets is much more open ended and intuitive to me—I collect hundreds of bits and pieces and images and photographs, and the ones that belong together seem to find each other, creating something far more than the sum of its parts. And while I'm working on a new project, ideas for an article I want to write or a design for a new handbag just pop right into my head.

I love making gifts, too. I also make jewelry for a living—which can be stressful, like any other job—but creating a gift or something for myself is still so much fun. I don't have to think about how much to charge, or churning out a few dozen of the same piece—just that my mom will love the necklace I'm making her, or that now I have something pretty to wear to my friend's wedding.

Like Cathy, I've felt such peace creating shrines to lost loved ones, especially during Day of the Dead (Dia de los Muertos). I make tributes to my father, my grandparents, my college boyfriend, and my dog, and adorn them with candles, fresh flowers, and the food and drinks they enjoyed. Though the tributes are displayed only one day a year, I feel such a connection to the people I miss so much.

TORIE

When my grandmother passed away, I decided to make a shrine in her honor. To come up with ideas for the objects to include in the shrine, I thought back through all of my memories of her, of the things she liked to do, and of the times we spent together. This process helped me focus on her life and put my energy into happy thoughts at a time when I felt so helpless.

As I gathered the objects and thought of new things to look for, I was comforted by memories of my grandmother and the feeling of her presence around me. Some family members contributed ideas: One relative sent me a charm of ballet slippers (my grandma was a dancer when she was young and had given her old ballet slippers to her). I was so grateful for the contributions and realized that shrine-making doesn't need to be an individual activity. It would be a great healing experience for a group of people to come together and each give objects for a common shrine, or each make their own shrine while they are all together as a group.

CRAFTS FROM THE PAST

RACHEL

As a kid, I was never a big fan of dolls. Once my dad came home from a business trip with a brand-new doll for me, and apparently I took it and threw it on the floor and sort of cursed it. Sorry, Pops! From an early age I regarded many dolls as slightly evil, especially the ones whose eyes opened and shut when you moved the doll body. My brother, on the other hand, went through a stage of being completely enamored with his doll. The boy doll had all of his parts, and when water was added to a little opening in his neck, he could pee all over everyone.

So, you may wonder why I chose to feature dolls from my past. As an adult, I continue to believe that most mass-produced dolls are evil, while I truly appreciate and love handmade dolls. My mom, the master needleworker, made me a Raggedy Ann doll for my seventh birthday; my great-grandmother created a doll in a pinafore dress for my mother's fifth birthday. I simply love the idea of a mother making a doll for her child and a grandmother making a doll for her grandchild. Doll-making may very well be a primal act, judging from immense collections of dolls from across cultures and across time housed in museums around the world. I think that doll-making and passing down dolls from generation to generation is a practice that we should revive. Why buy a creepy machine-made doll with terrifying flickering eyes (which most likely is produced in a sweatshop overseas by a child laborer), when you can make your own unique doll for your child?

CATHY

My mom made the most kick-ass doll clothes of all time. I don't know how she managed, as a single mom, to work full time, keep up with housework, and still sew tiny velvet bell-bottom jumpsuits

RACHEL

CATHY

SUSAN

TORIE

for my dolls. Mine were the best-dressed dolls in town. All my friends' dolls had those chintzy store-bought clothes that ripped easily and didn't fit right. My dolls had minidresses with reversible capes, fringed bell-bottoms, and wool suits. My mom usually salvaged scraps of fabric from clothes she made for me, so the dolls and I had matching wardrobes. One of her secrets was hidden on the inside of the rick-rack trim label: "Send three labels and fifteen cents postage and handling for a generous package of clippings suitable for trimming doll's clothes." If you look on the inside of labels today, you will find that inflation is the only thing that has changed: For three labels and four dollars, you can still order a generous package of trim clippings.

SUSAN

When I was little, I drew pictures all the time, especially (foreshadowing my future career as a crafty jeweler-seamstress) of the clothes and accessories I imagined wearing as a glamorous grown-up. The smiling girl in a snappy pink-and-blue ensemble that I drew twenty-five years ago looks eerily like me today—including an A-line skirt, legwarmers, and dangly earrings!

Some of my most treasured possessions are the dresses my grandmother sewed for herself when she was in college in the early 1940s. I also have the wrap skirts she made my mom, sundresses she made for me when I was little, and the clothes she sewed for my rag dolls. She did beautiful needle-point, too, and I inherited some of her unfinished pieces, which I hope to finish one day.

TORIE

When I was little my favorite book in the entire world was *Molly's Moe* by Kay Chorao. My mom and I would check it out from the library on a regular basis (probably much more than she would have liked)! It's a story about a girl whose favorite stuffed animal is a lizard named Moe. She takes him everywhere. One day, upon returning home from the supermarket, she can't find Moe anywhere and is upset at the thought of having left him at the store. It turns out that Moe was just in one of the grocery bags (sorry to spoil the ending for you!) and the two are happily reunited. I loved the story so much that my mom commissioned my great-aunt (who is an amazing seamstress) to create my very own Moe for me.

CRAFTY DISASTERS

RACHEL

One of my most traumatic crafting disasters took place on September 3, 2003, at 6:30 p.m. at a chain copy center that shall remain nameless. I walked in with a pile of books and vintage pictures along with several packs of shrink plastic. I inserted my credit card and loaded my shrink plastic into the paper tray. Listening to the hum of the copy machine as it scanned over my first image, a beautiful picture of a Russian showgirl dancer from the 1920s, I waited in anticipation for my shrink art to emerge. A smell seemed to erupt from the machine, red lights started to flash, and I'm not sure if this was a hallucination, but I swear I saw a small puff of smoke come out of the copier. Panic spread through me as a young employee came over to ask me if I needed help. She quickly moved towards the machine and pulled out the drum—a goopy mess covered with smoking, shrunk, shrink-plastic remnants. I could see part of the Russian showgirl's mouth melted onto the drum. It was mayhem. Red-faced, the young woman said she would need to "call this in" and went on to explain that these new machines heat up the ink before injecting it onto "normal copy paper."

I would like to use this opportunity to again apologize to this woman for ruining her drum, and hope that by sharing this experience in some way I have redeemed myself so that I don't go to copy machine hell.

CATHY

Working with resin has caused me more pain and suffering than you can imagine. If you don't measure and mix the two liquids just right, your whole batch is ruined. There are so many things that can go wrong. The resin can trap air bubbles, collect lint, or dry cloudy. I had just come off a long period of bad resin batches and didn't really know why, but suspected it was the chilly temperature of my new basement. It was a frustrating time, but it looked as though my luck was turning around as I poured a perfect, crystal-clear batch. As I stood looking in awe, my cat Jinx came out of nowhere and jumped onto the table. The belt buckles and magnets went flying and resin poured out of them all over the tray. My shrieks sent Jinx running through the basement and up the stairs, leaving wet resin paw prints all the way. After a second of being frozen in shock, I realized that the resin would be toxic to my cat if she licked it, and I quickly ran after her. I grabbed her, ran into the bathroom, and jumped into the shower with her in my arms. I gave her a full shampoo and scrubbed the resin out from between her kitty toes. She whined and squealed as she climbed the walls of the shower trying to escape.

After I took care of Jinx, I managed to salvage most of my resin-filled pieces. I used a toothpick to lift out the cat hair and refilled the empty ones with a newly mixed batch. It was one hell of a crafty disaster, but Jinx and I both learned from the experience: She doesn't jump on my worktable anymore, and I will *never* give her another bath.

On a funnier note:

After a long night of crafting at my house, my friend Suki spilled her family-size container of ultra-fine glitter as she got into her car. The next morning I came out to find my entire block sparkling in the sun. Each day, passing cars carried glitter farther and farther down the street. By the end of the week, I could see it three blocks away. This crafty disaster made us realize what a better world it would be if the streets were paved with glitter and that a little glitter goes a long way.

SUSAN

When I taught a class on making lip balms and bath salts a couple of years ago, I could only find one Pyrex measuring cup in the store kitchen for the two recipes I was demonstrating. Though I felt nervous about it, I melted the second batch of beeswax and sweet almond oil for vanilla-cinnamon lip balm in a heavy glass one instead. As I stirred the lip balm and went over the next steps with my class, the glass measuring cup exploded in the pan of boiling water and molten lip balm gushed everywhere.

I tried to stay calm and turned it into a chatty lesson on not using plain glass over heat. When I put the pan in the sink to get it out of the way without burning myself, the lip balm spilled out and thoroughly clogged the drain. I poured the first recipe's lip balms, washed the Pyrex cup, and managed to put together a replacement vanilla-cinnamon round in a few minutes while making small talk and (barely) resisting the urge to run out of the room. My students loved the lip balm, and the class ended well—

until I had to spend an hour afterwards unclogging the sink with two irritated store employees.

I wish I could say that was my only crafting train wreck, but due to a series of late-night near misses involving both iron and sewing machine, I am no longer allowed to sew after 10 p.m., no exceptions.

TORIE

Most of my crafting disasters involve me somehow messing up a project on one of the last few steps. From these mishaps I've learned many creative ways to disguise the mistakes . . . but sometimes things are just irreparable. In college I had taken a couple of jewelry-making classes at my university's craft center, an excellent facility with an entire room just for metalworking. Unfortunately for my short-lived metal-jewelry career, I moved up to Portland and was forced to say goodbye to the beloved craft center. I decided to enroll in a local jewelry-making class, located in a makeshift facility at a middle school. The supplies available to us were not in the condition that I was used to—there was no way to control the size of the flame coming out of the torches, the hammers had lots of dents and dings in them, and so on. I stuck with it, though, because I was really excited about making shiny silver jewelry.

I designed a ring that had a wide silver band topped with a beautiful purple and black stone. Every time I tried to solder part of it I would either melt it, or bend it, or ruin it somehow. It was frustrating, but I spent hours on it because I was determined to finish that ring. After four weeks of class, having worked on nothing but the ring, I was ready to solder the bezel cup (the part that holds the stone) onto the band. Once I attached that, I would only need to put in the stone and polish it up. Then I could finally wear my creation! I had spent a lot of time sanding the top of the ring band flat so the bezel would have a nice place to sit. I tried to solder it on, but couldn't get it to work. I was so afraid of bending the bezel wire or melting it and messing up the entire ring. So I asked the teacher if he would help me with it. He did . . . and as I stood there watching him, he bent it a little . . . then some more . . . and then completely melted it! It was totally past the point of repair! AAAH!!! I was devastated and didn't even go back for the last two weeks of class.

THE BEST + WORST ART SUPPLIES EVER

THE BEST

RACHEL

VINTAGE APPLIQUÉ

Walk into any thrift store and you will find what seems like an endless supply of vintage appliqué. The trick is knowing where to look. Beautiful hand-made appliqué often goes to waste when people discard tablecloths, napkins, and hankies. Many of these stained jewels in the rough can be found clipped to hangers in the linen section of your local thrift store. Vintage dresses are often covered with gorgeous appliqué, just waiting to be cut free from the polyester and reused on clothing, gift cards, and shrines. Take a peek in your grandma's and your mom's closets to see what you can unearth.

CATHY

RICK-RACK

I believe rick-rack to be a divinely inspired craft item. You can add it to absolutely anything (and believe me, I do) and transform that item into something amazing. You can sew it, glue it, or tie it. It comes in an insane variety of colors and is readily available both new and secondhand. Did you know that they even sell glow-in-the-dark rick-rack at Halloween? That one blew my mind. The sight of rick-rack brings me back to my childhood. Back then my mom sewed it onto just about everything (see Crafts from the Past on page 12). My second favorite art supply is pinking shears. I only mention them because I recently discovered that you can make your own fabric rick-rack with pinking shears.

SUSAN

FELT

I love felt—it is perfect for decorating or making patches and appliqués, children's toys, pillows, and anything else you dream up. It doesn't fray, it comes in a million colors, and it's really cheap. Cathy even found super cool glitter felt for her Show-Stopping Car Curtain (page 215). You can also wash old wool sweaters or blankets in hot water to create a heavier felt that's perfect for sewing hats or bags.

TORIE
RHINESTONES

A rhinestone here or there often adds that extra little sparkle that makes a project look complete. They can be added to anything from artist trading cards to handbags and hair barrettes. (Use them sparingly, though, to avoid gaudiness!) Oooh, sparkles!

THE WORST

RACHEL
TWO-PART EPOXY WITH SIXTY-MINUTE DRYING TIME

This glue slides around and I always manage to get a thin layer of the epoxy all over my hands. After I've scrubbed my hands obsessively until they look beet red and raw, the glue lingers and picks up dirt that I come into contact with and leaves a nice splotched sticky design that hangs on for days on end. To this day I don't know why people need a full hour to glue something together.

CATHY
NON-PERMANENT MARKERS

When you have a child, you have to hide those wonderful fine-tip permanent markers and accept the "washable" ones into your life. These childproof pens are completely useless except for the fact that they can be easily removed from the walls and from your kid's face. They smudge all over the paper as well as your hands, and forget about writing on anything shiny with them. My son is old enough to handle the permanent markers now and I have happily sent the washable ones on their way.

SUSAN
HOT GLUE

Though it is incredibly handy and does have many uses, hot glue has let me down time and time again. It really only works on porous materials like fabric—solid pieces like glass, plastic, or metal resist it. It's brittle and cracks under pressure, and you can get a hell of a burn from the tip of a hot glue gun.

TORIE
PLASTIC SNAP-ATTACHING TOOL

Never have I been as frustrated with a craft supply as when I tried using a plastic snap-attaching tool that I had to hammer. It did a good job of bending the snaps and *not* attaching them to the fabric! It's totally worth the extra money to splurge on the metal snap pliers.

MAKING IT SUPER CRAFTY

GETTING STARTED!

Welcome to our how-to section! We've put together 76 projects for you to try making—everything from pasties and legwarmers to shrines and cards. A lot of our projects have exact patterns and directions, but others are more open ended. We hope you'll be inspired to create your own unique pieces, too!

We've divided everything up into twelve chapters and included some handy 101 sections to get you started sewing, embroidering, making jewelry, sewing vinyl, and exploring the seductive world of shrink art.

We've also used a series of icons throughout the book. (See below.)

Here are some of the tools and materials we highly recommend having on hand:

GENERAL TOOLS

Good sharp **scissors** are a must!

Pinking shears add fancy detail with a vintage flair. These cool decorative scissors are an optional tool on many of our projects.

Decorative scissors in other patterns are fun to have on hand, too!

Jewelry pliers—see Jewelry 101 on page 52 for more details.

Grommet and snap pliers are a great investment with endless uses.

¼-inch standard hole punch is useful in many of our projects.

Easy or beginner friendly

Medium difficulty

Advanced or more involved

Kid friendly—for ages eight and up with supervision

Materials for the entire project will cost under $15

GLUE

Glue sticks are good for light paper projects and are very kid friendly.

Craft glue, such as Tacky Glue, dries clear and flexible.

Silicone sealer is perfect for paper or glass and is much thicker than craft glue, so it's handy for adding a glob to attach something oddly shaped, like a silk flower.

Hot glue guns can glue large, unusually shaped items and have a very quick drying time. But watch out: Hot glue snaps off easily and can give you one heck of a burn.

Strong glues, like E-6000 or two-part epoxy with four-minute drying time, are perfect for certain projects—whenever we list "strong glue," use one of these or a similar adhesive. *Warning:* These are very toxic and not kid friendly and should always be used with good ventilation.

Fabric glues are ideal for holding appliqués down as you sew them, or attaching an extra piece that won't be washed.

Note: Glue drying times vary from a few minutes to 24 hours—always consult the label before starting a project.

SEALERS

Decoupage medium, such as Mod Podge, is good for smoothly applying paper and adding a protective layer to your project. It comes in both matte and glossy finishes.

Matte medium is used to strengthen and seal surfaces of projects.

SEWING

See Sewing 101 on page 22.

WRITING, DRAWING, AND PAINTING

Sharp pencils

Fine-tip permanent markers like Sharpies are amazing for many things, especially drawing on shrink plastic.

A **notebook** with lined or unlined paper is handy for sketching or jotting down ideas.

Cardstock is perfect for making cards and pasties.

Acrylic paint is nontoxic, water based, and easy to use. Two coats on wood, fabric, or metal look a lot smoother than just one. Use a sealer (see above) to protect the surface.

Paintbrushes are great to have in a range of sizes, from tiny to huge.

Sponge paintbrushes are wonderful for applying paint or textured color on a variety of surfaces.

EXTRAS

A collection of baubles and trinkets like beads, found objects, rhinestones, jewelry pieces, small oddities, and vintage treasures are handy little extras to add when creating a shrine, collage, or handmade card.

THREADS

SEWING 101

HAND-SEWING

RUNNING STITCH

The running stitch is a quick way to mend or gather fabric into a seam. Simply weave the point of the needle in and out of the fabric at even intervals, always sewing forward, before you pull the needle through. The closer together your stitches are, the tighter and more permanent your seam will be. You can use a variation on the running stitch to hand-sew appliqués or decorations: Make your stitches very short (as seen from the top) with longer stitches (as seen from the bottom) between them, so your top layer is securely

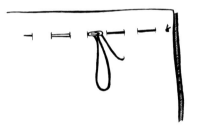

• If you do much hand-sewing, a thimble that fits your finger well is essential.
• Running your thread through wax (which comes in a handy plastic box) before sewing helps keep thread from tangling—honestly, it's a lifesaver!

attached, but the stitches aren't as noticeable on the right side of the design. The running stitch can also be used to embroider lettering or designs with the opposite approach: Make longer stitches on the top of the fabric to form the design and shorter stitches in between to anchor them on the back (see Embroidery 101 on page 274).

INVISIBLE STITCH

The invisible stitch is good for hemming and closing up openings in projects like sachets (page 49) and pillows (page 91) where you don't want the stitches to show. Once the hem or seam allowance is turned in and pressed into place, you'll be stitching on the inside of the fold. Start at one end of the opening and stitch back and forth between both sides of the seam allowance, just below the edge, being careful not to catch the outside fabric, until the opening is closed.

BACKSTITCH

The backstitch is a stronger, reinforced version of the running stitch. Instead of sewing a series of forward stitches, you backtrack to finish a stitch *behind* where your needle has emerged. Bring your needle up from the back of the fabric to the front, and make a stitch one length back, rather than forward. On the underside

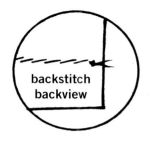

backstitch
backview

of the fabric, bring the needle up again a stitch length ahead to start your second stitch, and repeat the reinforced backward stitch. Sound confusing? See the diagrams!

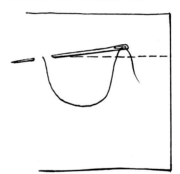

MACHINE-SEWING

Before you start a sewing project, make sure you are using the right needle for your fabric. Change your needles before each project to ensure your stitches will be even; needles become dull after a few hours of sewing. Use standard-point needles for woven fabrics and ball-point needles for silks, knits, and other stretchy fabrics.

WHICH NEEDLE?

Standard size: medium-weight fabric like standard cotton
Heavy duty: heavier, thicker fabrics like upholstery and canvas, or medium fabrics with fusible interfacing
Light: lightweight cottons, silks, and similar fabrics
Very light: sheer and delicate fabrics
Denim: denim and duckcloth
For tips on sewing vinyl, check out Vinyl 101 on page 226.

TENSION

Before you begin a project, test your tension on cloth scraps in a similar weight to the fabric you're using. As a general rule, thicker fabrics need a looser tension. Adjust your tension on your upper tension knob until both the bottom and top stitches lie flat and even and aren't too tight or loose.

STITCH LENGTH

As a rule, use longer stitches when basting or working with heavy material. Stitches tend to bunch up and are also hard to undo when they're too short. Medium-length stitches work well for most general sewing.

SEAM ALLOWANCES

For most patterns, seam allowances are ⅝ inch, which is marked (along with other lengths) as a guideline on your sewing machine's needle plate so you can follow it easily. You can use a seam allowance as small as ⅛ inch or as large as an inch; try narrow seam allowances for curves and smaller projects, and wider seam allowances for zippers and larger projects.

TAKING CARE OF YOUR MACHINE

Keep your machine covered when you aren't using it to keep it dust free and clean.

Always refer to your manual, but as a guide, clean out the bobbin area with a little brush after every 10–15 hours of sewing. Some machines may need a drop of oil applied to the bobbin area every month or so—but only when you are sewing frequently.

It's best to give your sewing machine an annual tune-up (usually $20–$50, depending on the type of machine you use). This is especially crucial for older models. Sewing repair businesses can service your machine and replace old or damaged parts. If you take care of your machine the way you take care of your car by giving it regular checkups and maintenance, it will run for years. Most repair shops also offer a twelve-month warranty on tune-ups, so you can bring it in for a free adjustment anytime in the year after your service.

• To sew around a corner, leave the needle in the fabric at the last stitch, lift the sewing machine arm, rotate the fabric to where you need it to be to continue sewing, then put the machine arm back down.

> Backstitch at the beginning and the end of your seams to secure your stitches.

• Always pull straight pins out just before you sew the seam—don't sew right over them! You can break a needle or the pin, either of which can fly into your face as you're sewing.

• Magnets can help keep your needles and straight pins in one place instead of all over your floor. Try putting a strip of magnetic tape on your sewing table in front of your machine to catch straight pins as you pull them out of your seams. Glue small button magnets on the underside of a saucer or small plate to keep pins in the dish, as kind of an open-faced pincushion.

• Pressing seams carefully as you sew garments makes your finished projects look professional.

• Keep a pair of small scissors handy on a long cord around your neck—essential for quickly snipping threads.

Backstitch at the beginning and the end of your seams to secure your stitches.

SEWING TOOLS

- **Seam ripper**, essential to fix a mistake quickly

- **Chalk or fabric pen/pencil**, to help measure when hemming skirts or pants

- **Sharp small scissors**, for trimming and small cuttings

- **Fabric glue or fusible sewing tape**

- **Pincushion** that fits on your wrist

- **Tape measure**

- **Iron**

- **Elastic/drawstring guide**

Happy sewing!

SUPER SOCK MONKEYS

YOU'LL NEED

One pair of socks

Stuffing (polyester, cotton, or old nylon stockings will work)

Embroidery thread for mouth and eyelashes

Buttons, felt, or embroidery thread for eyes

TOOLS

Scissors

Sewing machine (optional)

Needle and thread

Dowel or chopstick

Remember that cute monkey doll your grandma made for you out of a pair of socks? The sock monkey has been an iconic part of our culture since way back when, and now you can add your own style to this great old-school craft project. Use these instructions to make the old brown, white, and red favorite, or modernize your monkey with some colorful knee socks.

1. Turn both of the socks inside out. Imagine an invisible line that goes down the middle of sock #1 (see page 28). Now sew a seam ½ inch from the center line on each side: Starting about 3 inches from the edge of the heel, sew to the top of the sock and round off the ends (follow the dotted lines on sock #1 in the diagram). Cut the sock between the seams and to within 1½ inches of the edge of the heel. This is your monkey's head, main body, and legs.

2. Turn the sock right side out and use the opening in the crotch to stuff the head, body,

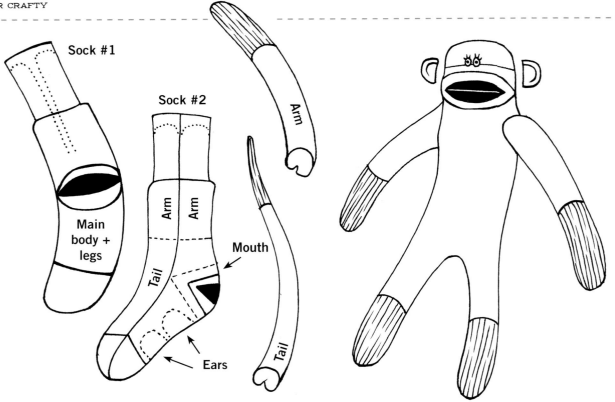

and legs. You can use a dowel or chopstick to make stuffing easier.

3. Cut the upper part of sock #2 into two pieces for the arms. Sew the seams right sides together, rounding one end and leaving the other end open to stuff. Turn the pieces right

side out, stuff them and hand-stitch them onto the body.

4. Cut the heel from sock #2, leaving an edge around the solid-colored part. This is the mouth. Hand-stitch the mouth onto the face, starting at the bottom. As you get to the top, add the stuffing and finish stitching it up.

5. Cut the tail in a 1-inch strip out of the remaining part of sock #2. Sew up the seam, right sides together, sewing one end to a point and leaving the other open for stuffing. Turn the tail right side out and stuff. Hand-stitch it onto your monkey.

6. Cut the ears out of the sole of sock #2. Sew up the edges, adding a little stuffing if you

like, and hand-stitch them onto the monkey's head.

7. Add the finishing touches like the mouth, eyes, and eyelashes using the embroidery thread, felt, and buttons. This part determines your monkey's personality. See the sidebar below for ideas.

Simply type "sock monkey" into any search engine, and a wealth of websites will pop up telling you everything you ever wanted to know about the little guy. You can even buy those classic brown, white, and red socks online.

Use the traditional red-heeled socks or go crazy with argyles. It's up to you! The size of your socks will determine the size of your monkey. Use different sizes to make an entire family. I used women's knee socks to make my striped monkey.

It's all in the eyes! You can create a person-ality for your monkey by simply changing the placement of the eyes and eyelashes. Eyes that are close together with lashes look sweet and

innocent while eyes that are farther apart with eyebrows look more sinister.

Remember that small objects like buttons can be a choking hazard for children under three: Use felt or embroidery instead.

Get creative with your monkey's outfits! I dressed Stella in a vintage doll dress that I found at a garage sale and then fancified with rick-rack trim. I made Jake's T-shirt out of a baby onesie that I found at a thrift store. I used the existing neckline, shoulder snaps, and wrist hem and cut it down to monkey size. Since the monkeys are pretty simple shapes, fitting a garment to them is quite simple: Just wrap the fabric around, cut where it looks like the seams should be, and sew the pieces together.

TATTOO FLASH PATCHES

YOU'LL NEED

Tracing paper

Fabric iron-on patches

One sheet of thin Styrofoam

Tape

Cool image the size of your patch

Acrylic paint

Newspaper

TOOLS

Pencil

Ball-point pen

Old rolling pin

Rubber printmaking roller

Scissors

8-inch by 10-inch piece of glass (you can use the glass from a picture frame)

This project puts a new twist on the iron-on patches that your mom used to patch the holes in the knees of your pants when you were a kid. Blank patches are available in an assortment of colors at most fabric stores. With a few other readily available art supplies, you can use clip art or your original artwork to make patches for your rock band, your secret club, or a special event.

1. Use a pencil to trace your image onto the tracing paper. Remember that when you print the image onto the patch, it will be a mirror image of what you started with. If you are using words, you will definitely want to scan or copy your image and flip it before you trace it. Also keep in mind that smaller details won't print as well as larger ones.

2. Cut a piece of Styrofoam the same size as your patch. You can cut the foam slightly smaller if you want to leave a border around the edge of your patch. Center the traced image on top of the foam. You may want to

I use acrylic paint because I like the consistency. However, if you plan to put your patch on clothing or something that you wash regularly, use fabric paint. Just make sure the paint is thick enough.

Sheets of thin Styrofoam are available at most art supply stores. You can also use the smooth side of the foam trays that come under meat and veggies at the supermarket.

The quality of your image will deteriorate as you print, but if you are careful with your foam blocks, you will get dozens of patches made before you have to retire them. It's called limited edition!

Remember to use lighter colored paint on darker patches and vice versa—the contrast will show your design better.

You can also use this method on paper to make cards, flyers, gift tags, stickers, and anything else you dream up.

For more block printing, try the Love Attack Block Print Card on page 265.

tape the paper in place to avoid shifting. Use a ball-point pen to retrace the image, pushing down slightly to leave an indentation in the foam.

3. Lift the tracing paper off the foam. If some of the details are not deeply indented in the foam, you can go over them with a pencil to make sure they are deep enough.

4. Prepare your workspace by putting down newspaper and having your sized patches set aside and ready to print.

5. Squeeze a ½-inch blob of paint onto the piece of glass. Use the rubber printmaking roller to spread it in an even layer on the glass as well as on the roller. Keep rolling until you notice the paint start to get thick and sticky. The paint will adhere to the patch better when it is slightly tacky. Roll an even layer of paint onto the carved foam piece, but don't overdo it. If you add too much paint, it will seep into the indentations and blur the image.

6. Place the foam, paint side down, onto the first patch piece. Smooth it into place and roll the rolling pin across it crosswise, then lengthwise, gently pushing down.

7. Peel the patch away from the foam. You are done! You can keep printing multiple patches with the same color by starting over at step 5. If you want to try the same image with a different color, simply wash your foam block with warm water, dry it, and start over with the new color.

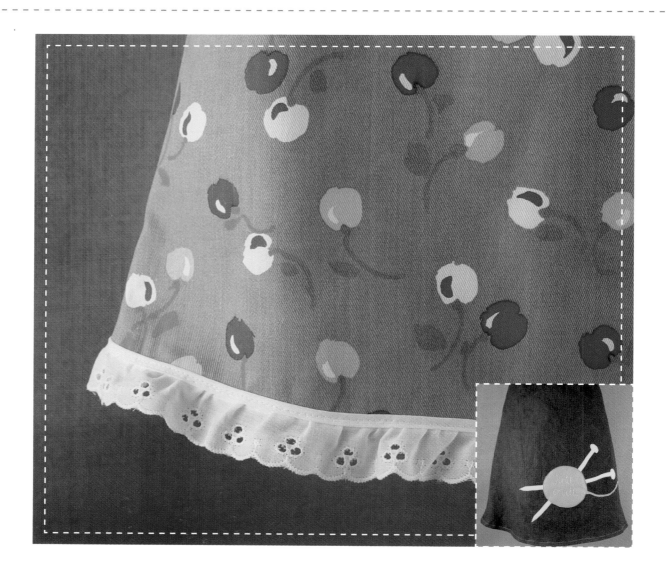

ONE-AFTERNOON SKIRT

BY SUSAN

YOU'LL NEED

A piece of stretchy material (for a 24-inch-long finished skirt with a 32-inch waist, I used a piece that was 54 inches wide and about 30 inches long)

An A-line skirt that fits you well as a guideline

Cotton thread in the same or contrasting color

1 yard of 3/8-inch-wide elastic

Lace, rick-rack, ribbon, or other decorative trims (optional)

TOOLS

Measuring tape

Sharp scissors

Pins

Sewing machine with a ball-point or stretch needle

Iron

Elastic guide (available at sewing stores) or a large safety pin

Needle (optional)

You can finish this adorable skirt in about an hour. Since it's elastic waisted, it doesn't need a zipper—it just pulls right on. Make it this afternoon and wear it out tonight!

1. Fold the material in half, with the finished (selvage) edges of the piece together, wrong side out. Put your guideline skirt down, flat and face up, so that one side is closest to the selvage edge and one side is closest to the fold. (See Fig. 1A.)

2. Cut around the outline of the guideline skirt, leaving an extra ½ to 1 inch of material on the sides and an extra 1½ to 2 inches on the top and bottom. This extra material will become the side seams, waistband, and hem.

3. You will end up with two trapezoid-shaped pieces, larger than the finished skirt will be, that will become the front and back of it. After you've cut out the two pieces, fold them down the middle to check the sides, top, and bottom for symmetry. This doesn't have to

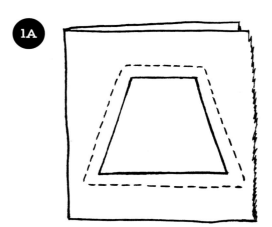

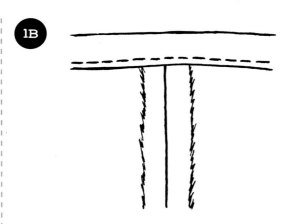

be extremely precise, but it's better to leave too much than too little—you can always tweak and narrow a skirt that's too big, but it's difficult to add fabric when the skirt is too tight or too short. Check to see that the flare will be roughly equivalent on each side and trim if necessary.

4. With the right sides of the two fabric pieces facing each other, pin each side together all the way down from top to bottom, using one pin every 3 or 4 inches. Set your sewing machine for a long or stretch stitch, so the stitches will stretch with the material. Stitch both sides with a ⅝-inch seam allowance.

Backstitch at the top and bottom of each side to hold the seam.

5. Press the two side seams open and flat on the inside, following the iron's instructions for the type of material you're using.

6. To start the waistband, fold the top ½ inch of material over to the inside all the way around, ironing it flat as you go. Then fold it over once again so there's a double thickness. Iron it flat again and pin it together every few inches. Starting at the side seam, stitch close to the bottom edge of the waistband (see Fig. 1B) all the way around, stopping an inch or two before you get back to the side seam so there's space to feed the elastic into the waistband.

7. Thread the elastic through the guide, or pin it with the big safety pin, and slide it into the waistband with your fingers guiding it from the outside. Guide it all the way around the waistband. When the elastic comes out the other side, pull it as tight as you desire, usually so it puckers just a little bit evenly all the way around. You can pin the elastic together and try on the skirt so the waist feels comfortable. If the waist is too big, try tightening the elastic.

8. When it fits well, sew the two ends of the elastic together securely either by hand or with the machine, making sure it lies flat and doesn't twist. Then machine-sew the last inch of the waistband closed, backstitching to hold the seam.

9. Make the hem the same way as the waistband, except that you'll sew all the way around without leaving an opening.

An appliqué (like one of the examples on the next few pages) is a perfect way to personalize your new skirt. I sewed a "Knit or Die" patch on a denim skirt, but you can try Tattoo Flash Patches (page 31), Field of Flowers (page 65), or anything else you like!

I love using eye-catching contrast stitching for the hem and waistband—like red thread on denim, or white on black. Adding one or two rows of lace or ribbon at the hem also gives good definition.

10. Pin the lace or other trim around the bottom of the skirt, if desired, overlapping it at a side seam. Sew it on using a medium-length straight stitch.

11. You're done!

An earlier version of this skirt how-to originally appeared on the fabulous **www.getcrafty.com.**

SUPER COOL APPLIQUÉS

BY SUSAN

YOU'LL NEED

Felt in desired colors

Fabric marker

TOOLS

Embroidery thread, needle, and 7-inch hoop

Scissors

Straight pins

Sewing machine or needle and thread

Make your own felt appliqués to decorate a handmade or store-bought bag, jacket, or skirt. I designed these knitting-themed appliqués for the One-Afternoon Skirt (page 35) and the Knit It! Bag (page 43), but you can use the same basic idea of cutting out and sewing your own felt shapes to celebrate your fondness for bicycles, chess, turtles . . . the sky's the limit. Best of all, unlike traditional appliqués that need to be sewn on with a tight zig-zag stitch, felt doesn't fray and can be attached using a much easier straight stitch—hooray!

Projects throughout the book incorporate appliqué—there's a list of other designs, as well as some pointers for hand-sewing, below the instructions. It's easier to machine-sew a patch or appliqué onto a flat fabric than a finished garment, but it can be done.

Some of these projects call for embroidery—check out Embroidery 101 on page 274 for tips. You can also create the same pieces with no embroidery if you like.

KNITTING APPLIQUÉS

1. If you want to embroider one of the slogans on your patch, do that first. Place a piece of felt in the 7-inch hoop. The patterns for embroidering "knit it!" and "knit or die" are outlined in Fig. 1A. Write your slogan by hand on your felt using a washable fabric marker—I handwrote mine in cursive, but feel free to design them (or any other phrase, for that matter) in your own style. Thread an embroidery needle with two 36-inch strands of floss, doubling it and knotting it at the end to make an 18-inch length.

knit
or die
knit
it! **1A**

2. Starting with the *K* of "knit," (see Fig. 1B) use a running stitch to create the letters of either phrase, left to right. Every five or six stitches, backstitch once to hold your embroidery in place.

3. To dot the *i* and finish the exclamation point, stitch an asterisk (pattern on page 276).

Hand-sewing felt appliqués works very well, especially if you're working with smaller patches or finished garments, which aren't as easy to use a sewing machine on (like the flowers on the Sultry Slip, page 141). Just attach them with small stitches about ¼ inch apart in a similar thread color, sewing around the perimeter of the appliqué.

4. Using the pattern in Fig. 2A, cut the yarn shape out of felt—centering the embroidery design, if you are using one, in the middle of the yarn ball and extending the tail off to the right. Cut two same-size needles out of the other felt color. (You can use a copier to enlarge the patterns to the correct size if you don't want to cut them freehand.)

5. Use straight pins to anchor the crossed needles on the fabric you are appliquéing. If you are using a sewing machine, set it for medium-length straight stitches and sew around the perimeter of one needle close to the

1B

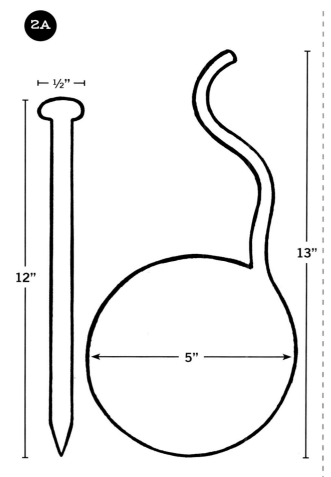

2A

⊢ ½" ⊣

12"

5"

13"

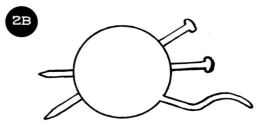

2B

edge, going more slowly around the curves. Repeat with the second needle. If you are sewing by hand, use small stitches spaced about ¼ inch apart to stitch the needles on, one at a time.

6. Position the yarn ball over the needles and sew it on the same way. (See Fig. 2B.) Voila!

STAR APPLIQUÉS
See the Superhero Slip + Boxers set for patterns, page 143.

FLOWER APPLIQUÉS
See Field of Flowers (page 65) for patterns. The Sultry Slip (page 141) and Charming Cloche Hat (see Four-Project Sweater, page 147) both use flower appliqués.

WHALE APPLIQUÉS
See the Whale of a Pillow (page 91) for patterns.

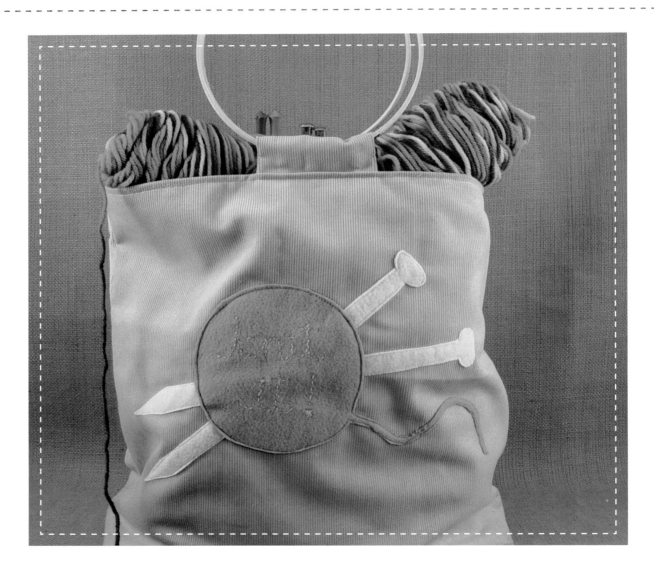

KNIT IT! BAG

BY SUSAN

YOU'LL NEED

1/2 yard sturdy outer fabric (we used pink corduroy)

1/2 yard lining fabric (any light- or medium-weight cotton will be fine)

Knit It! appliqué (see page 39)

Felt in one or two colors

8-inch by 14-inch piece of sturdy cardboard

Thread

TOOLS

Scissors

Straight pins

Sewing machine

Iron

Two 7-inch embroidery hoops (wood or plastic)

Needle

This roomy tote bag with embroidery-hoop handles and felt yarn-and-knitting-needles appliqué is a perfect project to try after you've been sewing awhile. If you need help getting started, check out Sewing 101 on page 22.

The Knit It! Bag is fully lined and features ingenious outside vertical pockets to hold straight needles of every size. Carrying your knitting and gear to a coffee shop or stitch + bitch has never been more stylish!

1. Using the pattern in Fig. 1A, cut out one bag piece in your outer fabric and one in your liner fabric. Cut out two 5-inch squares of outer fabric as well.

2. Following the instructions on the previous pages, make the Knit It! appliqué and sew it on one side of the outer fabric as shown. Skip this step for a plain bag or decorate it with your own Tattoo Flash Patches (page 31).

3. Cut three 4-inch by 12-inch pieces of felt (one in color #1 and two in color #2, if desired) and pin them to the other side of the bag, one inch apart, as shown in Fig. 1B. These will become the tall, skinny pockets for your needles. Sew them on, stitching from top to bottom, using a medium-length straight stitch on your sewing machine. To create a perfectly straight line, go slowly and keep a close eye on the seam. The first pocket will be sewn only along the sides and bottom edges. The second will have one extra seam down the middle to divide it into two pockets half the width of the first one. The third will have two extra seams down the middle, creating three even-skinnier pockets.

4. Fold the outer bag fabric as shown, right sides together (see Fig. 2A), pinning along both diagonal sides. Sew each side together, using a medium-length straight stitch, and backstitching at each end to hold the seam. Now pin the bottom seam together as shown in Fig. 2B and sew it together the same way.

5. Repeat step 4 with the lighter-weight fabric, sewing the seams the same way, to construct the lining of the bag.

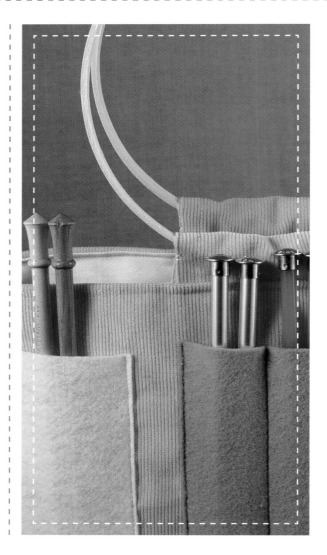

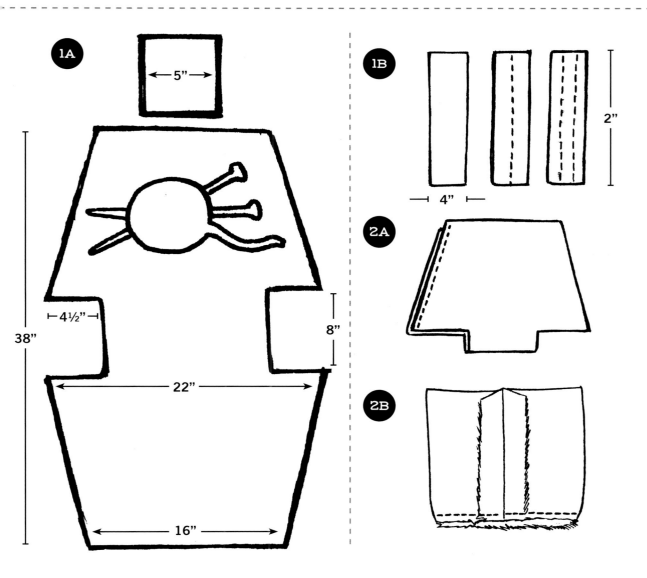

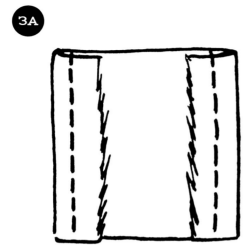

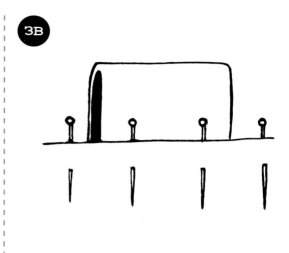

6. Turn the outer bag right side out and leave the lining wrong side out. Fold the raw edge on the top of the outer bag down ½ inch and use the iron (on a medium-high setting) to press it flat. Repeat on the lining piece. Place the piece of cardboard inside the bag so it reinforces the bottom.

7. Place the lining inside the bag, matching the side seams so they are lined up correctly. Pin the bag and lining together at the folded edge all the way around the top, so that the folded raw edge is tucked inside the two fabrics.

8. Fold and press ½ inch in on each vertical side of the 5-inch squares, as shown in Fig. 3A. Stitch to hem the sides of both squares. These two pieces will hold the handles on the bag. Fold them in half (see Fig. 3B) and pin them onto the center top of the bag with the raw edge tucked between the lining and outer fabric.

9. Stitch around the top of the bag, securing the folded fabric within the seam and backstitching at the beginning and end of the seam.

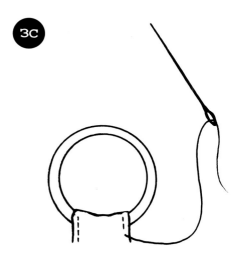

3C

10. Open one of the embroidery hoops by twisting the adjustable metal fastener on the outer circle until it opens. Set aside the inner circle. Guide the embroidery hoop into the fabric fold on one side of the bag. Twist the hoop closed and turn it so the metal fastener is hidden in the fabric fold. Repeat with the second embroidery hoop on the other side of the bag.

11. Use a needle and thread to hand-sew a few stitches at each side of the fabric fold to hold the hoop in place (see Fig. 3C).

12. Fill the bag with your knitting, needles, extra yarn, how-to books, and any other gear, and go out to craft night!

Check our Resources section (page 279) for books and websites with cool knitting patterns and tips.

Our love affair with felt continues throughout the book! Try Felt Flowers (page 67), Rock + Roll Kitty Toy (page 182), Superhero Slip + Boxers (page 143) or Show-Stopping Car Curtain (page 215).

SWEET SHOE BAG

SACHETS

SWEET SHOE BAG
+ MATCHING SACHETS

YOU'LL NEED

Small vintage pillowcase

Ribbon three times longer than the width of your pillowcase

TOOLS

Needle and thread

Sewing machine (optional, but recommended)

Putting your shoes or unmentionables in a pretty bag when you travel not only makes opening your suitcase a delight, but it also saves the embarrassment of displaying your personal items in plastic bags if your luggage gets searched at the airport.

SHOE BAG

1. Sew a straight line up the middle of the pillowcase, starting at the closed end (the bottom) and ending about an inch from the top. This will divide the pillowcase into two pockets and keep your shoes from rubbing together.

> Make a matching sachet with another vintage pillowcase or coordinating fabric.

2. Sew the middle of the length of the ribbon onto the center of the pillowcase about an inch from the top.

3. Place your shoes (one in each pocket), fold it in half, and tie the ribbon in a bow.

SACHETS

Put your fabric scraps to use and keep your dresser drawers smelling pretty! Sachets are easy to make and fun to give. My very first sewing project was Mother's Day sachets for the special ladies in my family, who all loved them! And even though my sewing skills have greatly improved, I still enjoy making sachets from time to time as gifts for my friends and family.

1. Pin the two fabric squares, right sides together, and sew around the square, leaving a 1-inch opening in the center of one side. Trim the corners.

2. Turn the square right side out and pull the corners out. Press as needed.

3. Fill the square with potpourri through the 1-inch opening to desired fullness.

4. Sew the opening closed using the invisible stitch. See Sewing 101 (page 22) for instructions.

YOU'LL NEED

Two 4-inch squares of fabric

Potpourri or fragrant dried flowers

TOOLS

Straight pins

Needle and thread

Sewing machine (optional)

Scissors

Iron

To personalize your sachets, embroider or appliqué letters or designs onto the fabric squares before you sew them together. Also try making your sachets in different shapes, like cats, dogs, or hearts. See Super Cool Appliqués (page 39) or Embroidery 101 (page 274) for ideas.

Experiment with different fillings—I like using dried lavender with rice for a French-countryside feeling. Place a sachet in your shoe bag to keep it smelling fresh.

JEWELS
+
BAUBLES

JEWELRY 101

With the right tools and a little practice, even a beginner can make beautiful wire jewelry.

TOOLS

Three kinds of jewelry pliers are good to have on hand:

Flat-nose pliers are for grasping, flattening, or forming angles.

Round-nose pliers are for forming loops and curves.

Wire cutters are for clipping wire.

You can get inexpensive pliers for about $6 each or really nice double-spring pliers for about $25.

Sterling silver and craft wire come in different gauges, or thicknesses. The larger the gauge number, the thinner the wire is, and vice versa. For the Granny Chic Sweater Clips project on page 79, we recommend 24-gauge, which is durable, but thin enough to use with small beads. Use thicker wire to form clasps or jump rings; for the S-clasps on the following page, heavier 16-gauge wire is best.

Craft wire is much less expensive than sterling silver—it's often silver-plated, but the plating can wear off in time, leaving it dull and gray. Sterling comes in two levels of firmness: half-hard and dead soft. Half-hard wire is best for making most jewelry—it has a spring and strength to it that dead soft doesn't have. You can use either craft or sterling silver wire for most projects, but sterling is wonderful to work with and lasts much longer.

TECHNIQUES

Before you start your first project, experiment with some of the basic techniques described below using craft wire. Spending some time getting comfortable with the basics now will help alleviate wire-related frustrations and feelings of general clumsiness once you start making your jewelry.

JUMP RINGS

The best way to open a jump ring is to twist the ring open, not to pull the sides away from each other. To do this, you'll need two pairs of pliers. Hold one side of the jump ring in one set of pliers with the opening at the top. With the other pair of pliers, grasp the other side of the ring. Slowly turn one hand toward your body while turning the other hand away from you.

To close the ring, twist it back and forth in the same motion you used to open it, moving your hands toward and away from your body, until the ring is closed again and snaps into place. Closing the ring with this motion ensures the strongest bond.

PLAIN LOOPS

(See Fig. 1A.) With pliers, bend a short tail of your wire at a 90-degree angle just above the bead or trinket. Using your round-nose pliers, hold the wire above the bend. Using your straight-nose pliers, wrap the tail of the wire around the nose of your round pliers (see Fig. 1B) until you've created a loop (see Fig. 1C). Trim any excess wire that extends beyond the loop.

WRAPPED LOOPS

(See Fig. 2A.) Start a wrapped loop as you would a plain loop, but use a longer piece of wire. Once you've wrapped the tail of wire around your round-nose pliers to form a loop, leave the excess wire tail extending beyond the circle. Hold the circle flat with your straight-nose pliers. (See Fig. 2B.) Grab the end of the wire tail with your round-nose pliers and carefully wrap it around the wire at the base of

the circle to form a coil. (See Fig. 2C.) Keep wrapping until you reach the top of the bead, and then trim the tail flush with the coil.

A **double-ended wrapped loop** (see Fig. 3) is simply a piece of wire that has a wrapped loop at both ends—and generally a bead or trinket in the center. You can connect a series of these loops to form a handmade chain.

S-CLASP

1. Cut a piece of 16-gauge sterling silver about 1½ inches long. Form a small loop at one end with your round-nose pliers (see Fig. 4A).

2. Grasping the wire about one third of the way down, bend it into a curve as shown in Fig. 4B. Now grasp the wire about one third from the other end and bend it into a curve there as well, forming an S (see Fig. 4C).

3. Make a small loop at the other end, like the one you made at the beginning. Using your pliers, adjust the S so one side is closed and one remains slightly open (see Fig. 4D). The closed side will connect to your necklace or bracelet with a wrapped loop or jump ring, and the open side of the S will

1. Practice, practice, practice!

2. Jump rings are really inexpensive, so if you distort one beyond repair, save yourself the frustration of trying to re-create a circle and throw it out.

3. Medium-gauge (22–26) wire is great for beginners: It is thin enough to bend easily, but not so flimsy that it bends all over the place and loses its form.

4. When you open and close a jump ring or work with wire, the metal becomes work-hardened and snaps neatly into place. But if you overdo it, the metal can become too brittle and break easily. Just start over with a new piece if you've had to adjust something over and over again and it's become fragile.

5. A perfect first jewelry project is drop earrings. Just form a simple loop at one end of a 3-inch piece of wire and slide on a bead, or a few beads. Make a wrapped loop at the top and put it on an ear wire. (You can use the same jump ring technique to open the ear wire loop.) Make a matching one and you have a pair of handmade earrings! We included a shrink-art earrings project on page 167, too.

form the hook of your clasp. Use it with a closed jump ring.

4. Don't worry if your first few clasps come out a little wonky—just keep practicing making the curves and loops, and you'll get it!

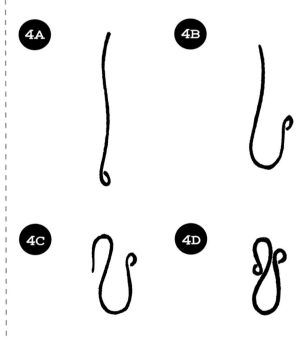

WONDER CUFFS

BY CATHY

YOU'LL NEED

Vinyl scrap, 1–2 inches wide and 8–9 inches long (your wrist size plus 2 inches is a good general rule)

Felt in contrasting color, the same size as your vinyl piece

One heavy-duty snap (this consists of four pieces)

Thread

TOOLS

Scissors

Pinking shears (optional)

Hole punch

Snap pliers

Sewing machine

FOR OPTION 2 YOU'LL ALSO NEED

Grommet pliers and grommets

FOR OPTION 3 YOU'LL ALSO NEED

A cool image you want to wear around your wrist, sized to fit on your cuff

A small piece of clear vinyl, 1/8 inch larger than the image

If you've ever dreamt of becoming a superhero who deflects bullets and lightning strikes with fancy wrist cuffs, this project is for you. With some scraps of vinyl or oilcloth (left over from the Viva Oilcloth Placemats on page 87) and some simple tools from the fabric store, you can make these fabulous cuffs.

For tips on sewing vinyl, check out Vinyl 101 on page 226.

1. Machine-sew your vinyl and felt pieces together all the way around the perimeter, wrong sides together. Sew about ¼ inch from the edge. If you plan to use pinking shears on the cuff, leave ⅜ inch at the edge. Trim the edges with either plain scissors or pinking shears to make them clean and neat.

2. Punch holes about ½ inch from the edge on both ends. Following the directions given with your snap pliers, apply the snaps over each hole, being careful to place them in the correct position to snap together.

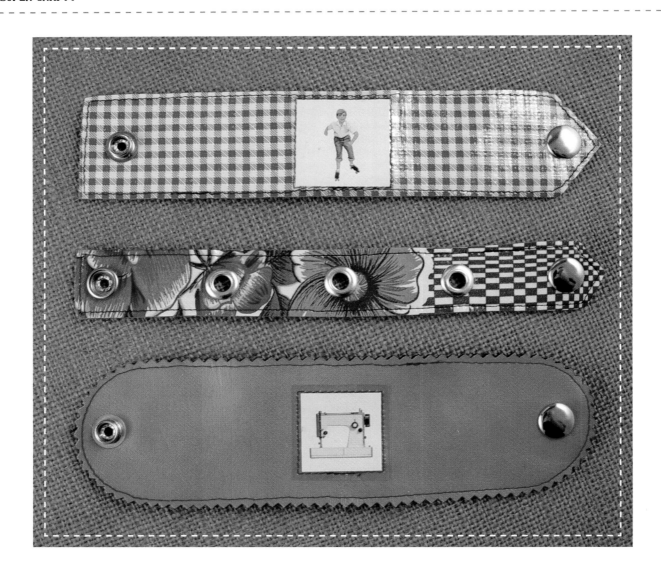

You can purchase grommet and snap pliers at most fabric stores for $15–$20. It might seem like a lot to spend on one project, but once you have them you will be adding snaps and grommets to everything you own! They are essential tools for any crafter.

3. If you want a simple cuff, you're done. Simple is beautiful!

4. Option #2 is to decorate your cuff with grommets. Use a pen to carefully mark where you want to place the grommets. Use a hole punch to make holes where you have marked.

Following the instructions included with your grommet pliers, place the grommets in the designated holes. Fancy!

5. Option #3 is a bit more complicated but very cool. You will need to sew the image onto the vinyl piece *before* you sew on the felt backing. Carefully center your image under the clear vinyl cover and place it onto the vinyl wrist piece. I placed tape on the very edge of the clear vinyl piece to hold it in place while I carefully sewed around the image. Follow steps 1 and 2 above to complete your cuff.

6. Put your cuffs on and deflect lighting bolts!

PASTIES FOR EVERYONE!

VINTAGE BETTIE

LADYBUG LOVIN'

SUPERSTAR

FLIRTY FLORAL

LES FLEURS SONT POUR TOI

VINTAGE BETTIE PASTIES

YOU'LL NEED

Two circles of leopard fabric, each 3 inches in diameter

Two circles of red felt, each 2-1/2 inches in diameter

Four fabric leaves on wire

Four fake cherries on wire

Fabric glue

Two pieces red mini rickrack, each 7 inches long

Two pretty vintage buttons

Toupee tape

TOOLS

Scissors or pinking shears

Hot glue gun

I used to work at a costume shop located near the red light district that catered to a large clientele of exotic dancers. One of my first projects there was to add Velcro to a gown so it could be ripped off quickly and easily. I also made lots of pasties. I had so much fun working there, and I'm thrilled that my pastie-making skills have finally come in handy. This pair has a vintage flair, reminiscent of the pinup girls of the '40s and '50s.

1. Cut a wedge out of both the leopard fabric and the felt circles. If the circles were a pie with eight pieces, you would cut out one pie piece (see Fig. 1A). You will join the two sides where the pie piece was taken out (see Fig. 1B) to form a cone shape (see Fig. 1C). But first, get the fruit arranged and ready to glue.

2. Take two leaves and two cherries and arrange them as you want them to hang on the front of the pastie. Twist the wires together to hold them in place. Put the wire ends through the middle of the leopard circle and hot-glue

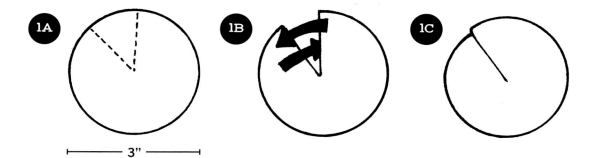

them flat against the backside of the fabric. Overlap the two sides slightly to form the cone shape and hot-glue them together. Arrange the leaves and fruit to cover up the seam. Repeat with the second leopard circle, cherries, and leaves to make pastie #2.

3. Straighten out the wires glued to the backsides so that the cones are straight and even. Add the felt lining to the backs so that the wires won't poke you. Test out how the felt pieces fit into the back of the pasties. You may have to trim the edges a bit to make them fit perfectly. Form a cone with the felt circle by hot-gluing the edges together, then glue the whole thing into the back of each pastie.

4. Use fabric glue to attach the rick-rack trim in a circle around the front of each pastie, about ¼ inch from the edge.

5. Use hot glue to attach the pretty buttons to the very center of each pastie.

6. Trim the outer edge of the leopard fabric with pinking shears for a nice finishing touch.

7. Stick them on with toupee tape and have fun!

I found my fake leaves and cherries at an estate sale—the source of some incredible craft supplies. Way back when, getting crafty wasn't a hobby, it was a way of life. Fake fruit and foliage are also easy to find at most craft stores.

FLIRTY FLORAL PASTIES

YOU'LL NEED

Two circles of cardstock
(3 inches in diameter)

Craft glue

Approximately 20 small
and medium-sized silk
flowers

Approximately 10 tiny and
extra-small silk flowers

Rhinestones (if desired)

Toupee tape

TOOLS

Scissors

Fashioned after vintage bathing caps, these flirty floral pasties add a touch of spring to any dull day.

1. Create two 3-inch pastie forms out of cardstock following step 1 in the instructions for Vintage Bettie Pasties (page 59). Use craft glue instead of hot glue to join the sides.

2. Pull the silk flowers off their stems. Trim any remaining stem off the back of the flower so that nothing sticks out. Sometimes the center of the flower falls out—if it does, that's a great place to glue a rhinestone or another bauble!

3. Divide your silk flowers in half; arrange half of them on one pastie to determine your layout and exactly how many flowers you will need.

4. Once you've decided on your design, start attaching the largest flowers by dabbing craft glue on the back of each one, then placing them one by one on the pastie. Hold each flower in place for a few seconds or so while the glue sets. Keep adding flowers until the entire pastie form is covered. Allow glue to dry.

5. Repeat step 4 for the other pastie.

6. Use the tiny flowers for covering up little gaps in your arrangement of the larger flowers, or just for more decoration. Dab glue on the back of each tiny flower and then place it. Allow them to dry.

7. Place some toupee tape on the back of each pastie and stick 'em on!

SUPERSTAR PASTIES

These starry pasties instantly transform any girl into a nighttime superhero!

1. Follow the instructions for Vintage Bettie Pasties (page 59) to create a cone shape out of each circle of cardstock, using craft glue instead of hot glue.

2. Add six star stickers to each one, spacing them out evenly, so they circle the edge of the pasties.

3. Put a generous amount of silicone sealer on the tip of each cone and place a star cut-out on each one. Let the glue set for at least an hour.

4. Be a superstar!

YOU'LL NEED

Two circles of red cardstock (3 inches in diameter)

Craft glue

12 silver star stickers

Silicone sealer

Two stars cut out of metallic silver cardstock (1-1/4 inches in diameter)

TOOLS

Scissors

BY SUSAN

LES FLEURS SONT POUR TOI

BY RACHEL

YOU'LL NEED

Vintage appliqué

Small black feathers

Craft glue

Mini rhinestones

Toupee tape

TOOLS

Scissors

Toothpick

You are planning a romantic evening with your special someone and your mind is wandering . . . and suddenly you must search for a semimatching, sexy yet slightly understated bra and panty set. Panic and extreme displeasure set in as you rummage through your drawers and toss around bras and panties that should have been retired last year. Stop and listen to that superhero voice inside your head! It's the pasties mantra: Pasties for Everyone! What better way to top off your romantic evening than with a special, private viewing of your own handmade pasties?

1. Go to your local thrift store's linens section and look for vintage appliqué flowers on pillowcases or tablecloths.

2. Cut out two flowers for the base of your pasties.

3. Glue feathers onto your appliqué as desired.

4. Dip your toothpick in the craft glue and place a small glue dot on the feather and glue on a mini rhinestone. Repeat this step on the feathers and appliqué until you have glued on rhinestones as desired.

5. Attach a ¼-inch piece of toupee tape on the back of each pastie, put them on your boobies, and go to town!

LADYBUG LOVIN' PASTIES

The trick to making a slammin' set of pasties is to express an aspect of your personality. The Ladybug Lovin' pasties are for the silly, playful girl who definitely doesn't take herself too seriously. These pasties are a perfect springtime treat for someone special!

1. Go to your local craft or scrapbook store and look for small metal discs and paper ladybugs. If you cannot find metal discs with holes, you can substitute heavy cardstock. If you use cardstock, you will need to cut two circles out of the cardstock and buy a small hole punch to create the holes around each circle.

2. Dip each small

YOU'LL NEED

Small red feathers

Craft glue

Two metal discs with small holes

Masking tape

Paper ladybugs

Mini red rhinestones

Toupee tape

TOOLS

Scissors

Toothpick

When I purchased the ladybugs and metal discs, the woman working feigned interest in my project and fulfilled the craft store's mandate to *always* ask what customers are making. While I usually answer, "I don't know," this time I said, "I'm making my own pasties as a surprise for my husband." I got the stink-eye as I left the store. Too bad, because she really could use a pair of pasties herself, instead of all that turquoise pancake eye shadow!

feather into craft glue and glue into each hole of the two metal discs. You may want to secure the feathers with masking tape on the back of each disc until they dry.

3. Glue a ladybug to the center of each metal disc.

4. Dab on a small dot of glue with a toothpick to glue on a rhinestone. Continue this step until you have glued on your desired number of rhinestones.

5. Let your discs dry for one hour.

6. Attach a ¼-inch piece of toupee tape to the back of each pastie.

7. Go for a spring frolic!

FIELD OF FLOWERS

Felt and oilcloth flowers are instant-gratification projects—they're quick to make, very addictive, and make perfect gifts or accents for your wardrobe. The styles pictured are just suggestions to get you started—try designing your own flowers in every color and size!

Felt is available in small pieces at any craft store, but for the best selection of colors, try a bigger fabric store—you can even buy it by the yard. Vintage buttons and beads are cheap and plentiful at yard sales and thrift stores and make lovely flower centers.

Oilcloth flowers are also really fun to make—and they're waterproof and super durable, so they can decorate sturdier things, like raincoats, messenger bags, belts, or hats. Oilcloth comes in gorgeous bright colors and graphic designs, and mixing patterns creates a bold, lively accent. Ordinary sharp scissors and pinking shears cut oilcloth beautifully and, like felt, the edges don't fray.

FELT FLOWERS

OILCLOTH FLOWERS

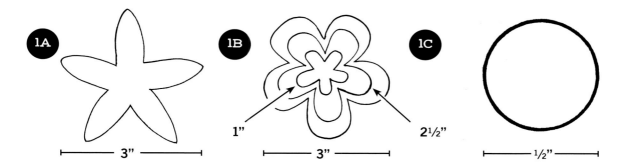

YOU'LL NEED

Felt in at least two different colors

Thread

Pinbacks or safety pins

Buttons, beads, charms . . . whatever you want to use to decorate your flower

Craft or fabric glue, if you don't want to sew

TOOLS

Sharp scissors

Pinking shears (for the small flower)

Sewing needle

FELT FLOWERS

1. Cut a few flower shapes out of felt, in contrasting colors or sizes if you like.

• For the white daisy, cut out two daisy shapes (see Fig. 1A) from the white felt and a ½-inch circle from the yellow felt.

• For the pink and red flower, cut one each of the largest shape in light and dark pink felt, one of the medium-size shape in red, and one of the small size in dark pink, from Fig. 1B.

• For the small pink and green flower, cut a 1-inch circle out of pink felt with pinking shears and a ½-inch circle out of green felt, as in Fig. 1C.

2. Layer the flower pieces, angling the shapes so all the petals show. If you use different sizes, the largest cut-out piece will be the back of your flower pin. Secure them with a few tiny stitches, pulling the needle and thread through back to front so the knot is on the back.

3. Position the pinback on the back of the flower and secure it with stitches through the holes. If you're using a safety pin, just secure the closed side of the pin to the back with four or five small stitches.

4. To add beads, sew them on with tiny stitches, clustering them in the center—or make up a pattern of your own. Secure with a double knot on the back.

5. If you don't want to sew, you can glue the layers together instead of stitching, following the same general directions for layering. Let your flower dry for at least two hours before pinning or wearing it out!

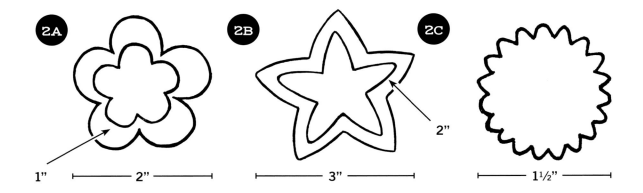

2A 1" 2"

2B 3" 2"

2C 1½"

For flower hair clips, use bobby pins or barrettes instead of pinbacks! Glue the finished flower on a wider hair clip or secure it to a clip with a few stitches and then seal the placement with a drop of craft glue.

To decorate a handbag or piece of clothing (like the Sultry Slip on page 141), just stitch the flower in place directly on the bag or garment. Try multiple flowers of different sizes or colors together, too! (To keep the flowers staying fresh after you sew them on, hand-wash the clothing instead of putting it through the washing machine—the felt will pill with too much wear.)

YOU'LL NEED

Cardstock for the flower patterns

Oilcloth in at least two different colors

TOOLS

Pencil

Sharp scissors

Pinking shears

Grommet pliers and grommets

OILCLOTH FLOWERS

1. For the smaller two-layer flower, draw the two shapes from Fig. 2A on cardstock and cut them out. Place the patterns on the wrong side of the oilcloth and trace them with a pencil. Cut out the shapes and layer them together— we used bright yellow and red oilcloth for contrast, but you can choose any colors or designs you like. You can also cut flower shapes out freehand if you'd like.

2. For the larger three-layer flower, follow step 1 to cut out the three shapes from Figs. 2B and 2C. Use pinking shears to cut the center shape. Layer them together so all the petals show.

3. Use grommet pliers to attach the flowers to a bag, garment, or anything you like! To make a striking choker, add one flower to a wide piece of grosgrain ribbon, placing the flower off center for a lovely effect. Add a snap with the grommet pliers to clasp the choker in the back.

BEJEWELED + BAUBLED PURSE

BY RACHEL

YOU'LL NEED

Vintage leather or vinyl purse

Vintage Lucite and glass beads

Vintage rhinestone brooches

Vintage cabochons

Newspaper

Paper

Strong glue

Clear tape

Decoupage medium

Two to three bags of microbeads (black or your preferred color)

Sealer

TOOLS

Scissors

Rubber gloves

Breathing mask

Paintbrush

If you are a big fan of vintage beaded purses, this project is for you. If you're an obsessed thrift store shopper like I am, every once in a while you will run across that spectacular find of an intact beaded purse (if you're lucky). More often you'll find old beat-up vinyl, leather, and fabric purses. You'll also discover plenty of old-lady necklaces and random broken jewelry parts in thrift store purgatory bins. What happens when an old purse meets up with granny beads? You are about to find out.

Choose a pattern and color scheme that will perfectly complement your personal retro style.

1. Go to your local thrift store and pick out a vintage vinyl handbag or clutch of your choice.

2. Choose a flat surface with lots of work space. I usually like to use the floor, but a table will do just as well. Cover your surface with newspaper. This will protect your floor or table from glue droppings and runaway beads.

3. Collect all of the vintage beads, brooches, and any other charms or jewelry parts that you plan to include in your purse design.

4. Take a piece of paper and cut out a shape the size of your purse. Then spend some time arranging your jewelry components on paper to explore the design possibilities. Sometimes it's good to create a design, let it sit overnight, and come back the next morning to see if you still like it.

5. Once you have created your fabulous retro design, it is time to go to town.

6. Put on your rubber gloves and mask. Cover the back of each jewelry component, one at a time, with a thick layer of strong glue.

7. Begin gluing your jewelry components, one by one, onto the handbag surface. For best results, apply glue on both the back of the jewelry piece and on the part of the purse where you will be placing it, and then wait 1 minute for the glue to begin to harden before you put it down. This will increase the stickability of each item.

8. Press your first piece onto the purse surface, and then secure your item onto the purse with a strip of clear tape so that it doesn't slip while the glue hardens.

9. Repeat steps 7 and 8 until you have completed your purse design.

10. Set your purse aside someplace where it won't be disturbed and wait for the glue to harden for 24 hours—after that, you can remove the tape.

11. With a small paintbrush, paint all remaining visible surfaces with a thick layer of decoupage medium. Then carefully sprinkle your microbeads over those areas, covering every tacky surface. The microbeads, which come in a variety of colors, will give your purse a beaded look in the spaces between your jewels.

12. Let your handbag sit for 1 hour until the sealer dries, then lift your purse to remove excess unglued microbeads. Make sure to carry out this step on top of your newspaper or you will be living among pesky microbeads for months.

You can choose a different background embellishment for your purse. Glitter, vintage fabric, or vintage pictures can be collaged onto the surface of the purse with craft glue and matte medium. Add vintage beads, buttons, and rhinestone jewelry pieces to your background with craft glue. Need a smaller purse or clutch? You can also choose a tired-looking clutch or coin purse from your own closet or local thrift store to bejewel to complement your wardrobe.

13. Repeat steps 11 and 12 for areas where the microbeads didn't stick. Don't worry—you are bound to miss a few spots the first time around.

14. Wait another hour and then coat the surface of the entire purse with sealer to protect all your hard work and to create a uniform sheen. Allow at least 2 more hours of drying time before you hit the town with your new retro handbag.

RETRO FLAMENCO TIARA

YOU'LL NEED

18-gauge wire from the hardware store

Vintage or new thick velveteen

Styrofoam head (optional)

Thin cardboard or cardstock

Vintage felt hat or thick new felt

Acrylic paint (optional)

Colored paper

Craft glue

Rhinestones

Decoupage medium

TOOLS

Wire cutters

Sharp scissors

Needle and thread

Sewing machine (optional)

Pencil

Straight pins

Toothpicks

Paintbrush

I've always had a secret desire to dance the Flamenco—and to own a tiara, except I never could find the right tiara among all the ultragirly rhinestone ones. So all you edgy girls who hanker for a tiara, this project is for you! Wear it to your favorite punk rock band's next show, to the gallery opening this weekend, or to a special holiday party.

PART A: CREATE THE BASE

1. Wrap a piece of wire around your head at forehead level to create a loop. Add 1 inch to the end of your loop and cut it with the wire cutters. Bend the loop back into a straight piece of wire. Cut a 1-inch-wide strip of velveteen the length of your wire. Fold the velveteen in half, right side out, and sew it into a long tube. You can hand-sew the tube or use a sewing machine. Run the wire through the sewn tube and form it into a circle. Push the velveteen down the wire on each side, exposing the ends of the wire. Twist the wire ends together until you have created a secure closure to your wire loop. Pull the velveteen up on each side and sew the ends together to complete the velveteen circle that will fit around your head.

2. Create another long tube of velveteen and run another piece of wire through the tube—I suggest using a piece 3 to 5 feet long to give yourself plenty of space to get fancy with your wirework. For my tiara I created a wire mockup design on a Styrofoam head. If you are not already the proud owner of one of these heads, you can borrow your friend's head or use your own head in the mirror. Now you can explore some simple wire-sculpting techniques to create the sides and top of your tiara. (See Fig. 1 for wire-wrapping ideas.)

PART B: FASHION FELT SHAPES FOR THE FRONT

3. Cut out three to five 3-inch-square pieces of cardstock. Using a pencil, draw out a winged shape (or a shape of your choice) that will be a repeating design on the front of your tiara. You are making your own pattern that you will use for all of your felt shapes. Experiment with several different shapes until you find one that speaks to your inner tiara-wearing self.

4. Pin the cardstock pattern onto your felt and cut out your shape. Repeat this step until you have cut out a desired number of shapes—I cut out three for my tiara. I highly recommend using an old felt hat. The felt is already stiff and will easily sit upright or in any desired position without much maneuvering. If you are using new felt, see step 5.

5. To attach the felt shapes to your wire base, sew each one onto the wire-covered velveteen in the desired positioning. I hand-sewed my felt shapes onto the wire frame in a layered design. I used thick vintage felt, which curves upward from the base of the tiara. I hand-sewed wire to the back of some of the felt pieces so they'd stand upright, which adds height and drama to the tiara.

6. To mask the wire, either paint over it with acrylic paint or cut out small strips of felt and glue the strips over the wirework.

PART C: ADORN WITH FLOWERS AND OTHER SHAPES

7. Sketch out flower shapes on the colored paper. You can also photocopy flower shapes from books, magazines, or postcards, or print out images you find online. Once you have sketched or pinned a flower design on your colored paper, cut out the design with small sharp scissors. Repeat this step until you have the desired number of flowers to adorn your tiara.

8. Glue the paper flowers onto the felt shapes using craft glue. Allow 20–30 minutes drying time.

9. Use a small paintbrush to apply a layer of decoupage medium over each of your flower shapes. The sealer will protect your paper shapes, increase their durability, and create a uniform sheen over all of your paper work. Allow 30 minutes drying time.

PART D: BEJEWEL YOUR TIARA

10. Your tiara may not be complete without a few rhinestones! I suggest using rhinestones that already have a sticky surface on the back. (You can find them at beauty supply, craft, and scrap-booking stores.) Carefully push the rhinestones into the wire frame and/or the felt to add a finishing sparkly touch. If you can't find the sticky rhinestones, use a toothpick to apply craft glue onto the back of each rhinestone, then stick away.

11. Crown yourself and go have fun!

CRAFTY CLIP

PINK + GREEN SPARKLES

BY SUSAN/TORIE

GRANNY CHIC SWEATER CLIPS

These darling little chains adorned with beads, charms, and dangles hold a cardigan sweater, coat, or jacket together, or look equally good decorating a handbag or pocket. They're addictive to make—once you finish one, you'll need more in every color combination!

We ordered our clips from Rio Grande (see Resources on page 279), found our chain at the hardware store, and got our beads and charms at thrift shops and bead stores. The first clip uses dangling beads and charms, and the other has beads wire-wrapped as part of the chain. See Jewelry 101 (page 52) for plenty of help with the wire instructions.

Each design also calls for specific beads and charms, listed below with each set of instructions. Or, make up your own combinations!

PINK + GREEN SPARKLES

1. Cut a 7-inch length of chain. Cut a 3-inch piece of craft wire and use the round-nose pliers to form a simple loop at one end. Put a

YOU'LL NEED

Base metal chain (approximately 7 inches for each one)

24-gauge craft wire

Beads, charms, or other trinkets

Small jump rings

2 clips

TOOLS

Round-nose, flat-nose, and wire clipper pliers

FOR PINK + GREEN SPARKLES YOU'LL ALSO NEED

3 larger beads (I used pink)

4 smaller ones (I used green)

Clear seed beads

FOR CRAFTY CLIP YOU'LL ALSO NEED

Alphabet beads to spell "crafty" (or the word of your choice)

clear seed bead on the wire, then a pink bead, then a second clear seed bead. Bend the wire to form a right angle ¼ inch above the beads to hold them in place. Repeat with the other six beads.

2. Lay the chain flat on a tray or plate and arrange the beads in the pattern shown, spacing them three links of the chain apart.

3. Attach each bead dangle to the chain with a wrapped loop.

4. Open two jump rings and use one to connect the first clip to one end of the chain. Repeat with the second one.

CRAFTY CLIP

1. Cut your base metal chain so you have five single links and two pieces with two links.

2. Use one jump ring to attach one of the two-link pieces of chain to one sweater clip. Repeat with the other jump ring, two-link chain, and sweater clip.

3. Cut six 3-inch pieces of craft wire.

Other charming projects to ornament yourself with include Pasties for Everyone! (page 58), shrink jewelry and shoe clips (pages 159–179), and the Gingham Delight Belt (page 233).

4. Lay out your design on a plate or tray so the clips are on each end and the alphabet beads each have one single link between them.

5. Attach each alphabet bead (in the order they appear in your design) to the chain links. Place each alphabet bead on a piece of 3-inch craft wire and form a wrapped loop on each end, making sure the chain link is in the loop before you wrap it closed. (Attach the left end of the first letter and the right end of the last letter to the double-linked chain and clip).

PRETTY PAPER + FABRIC JEWELRY

With a little decoupaging, you can turn your favorite art paper, wallpaper, or fabric into wearable art. This is a fun and easy project with limitless possibilities!

YOU'LL NEED

Decorative paper or fabric

Aluminum foil or wax paper

Decoupage medium

Rhinestones, if desired

Craft glue

Ribbon

Two crimp beads with a loop on one end

Clasp (see Jewelry 101 on page 52 to make your own)

One jump ring (if needed for attaching clasp)

TOOLS

Scissors

Foam brush or paintbrush

Flat-nose pliers

Fabric measuring tape (optional)

NECKLACE

1. Find paper or fabric with images that you would like to use for your jewelry. Color copy the image(s) if you need multiples. Then cut out your designs.

2. On aluminum foil or wax paper, lay your images face down and paint a coat of decoupage medium on the back of each one. Gently move the cut-outs to a clean part of the foil or paper. Allow them to dry. (Moving them to a clean part of the paper will help keep them from sticking. If they do stick when dry, gently peel them off the work surface and trim off any excess decoupage medium with your scissors.)

3. Flip the cut-outs over and paint one coat of decoupage on the front of each image. Again,

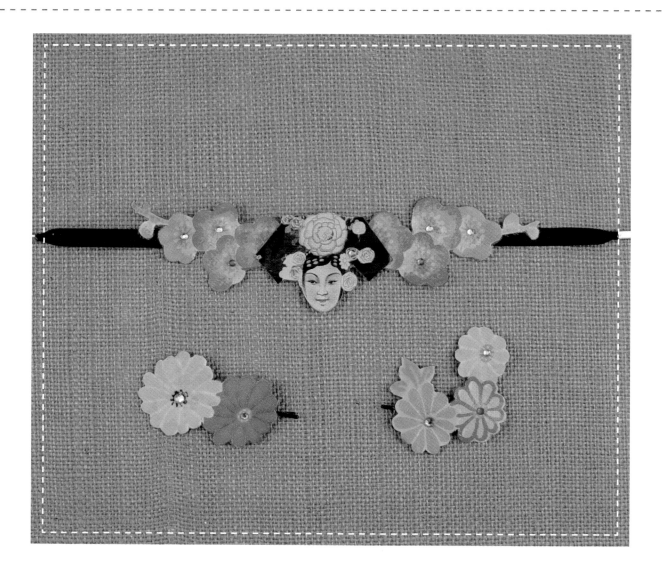

move the cut-outs to a clean part of the work surface to prevent sticking. Allow them to dry.

4. Repeat steps 2 and 3 as necessary, until the paper or fabric is of desired thickness and sturdiness. (For this necklace I used three coats on the front of the paper, two on the back, and two coats on the front of the fabric, one on the back.)

5. If you want to spice up your necklace with rhinestones, glue them onto your cut-outs wherever you like. Allow the glue to dry.

6. While the glue is drying, determine the length of your necklace—either by measuring your neck or wrapping the ribbon around your neck and cutting it to the desired length.

7. Place one end of the ribbon in a crimp bead. Hold it in place with one hand while using your pliers to push each side of the clamp down over the ribbon. Repeat for the other end of the ribbon. (Be sure to fold the crimps down on the same side of the ribbon on both ends.)

This inexpensive gift is fun and easy to make!

To make hair clips, follow steps 1–5. Then glue the images onto bobby pins or hair clips.

If you don't want to use glue, try sewing your cut-outs onto the ribbon. The stitching can become part of the decoration.

Experiment with different types of jewelry—bracelets, earrings, or pins—and find new ways to adorn yourself with paper!

For another fun project using decoupage medium, try the Glowing Glass Candleholder on page 247.

8. Using pliers, attach each piece of the necklace clasp to the clamp beads. You may need to use a jump ring to attach the clasp to your clamp bead. For wire jewelry techniques, see page 52.

9. Choose where you would like the paper or fabric cut-outs to be on the ribbon necklace and glue them in place. Allow the necklace to dry, and then try it on!

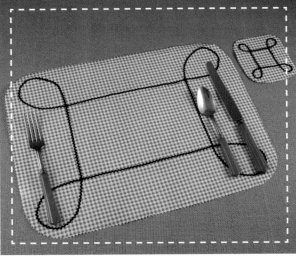

VIVA OILCLOTH PLACEMATS + COASTERS

YOU'LL NEED

1 yard of 36-inch-wide oilcloth

1 yard of contrasting oilcloth (only if you are making double-sided placemats and coasters)

Rick-rack (optional)

TOOLS

Pencil

Scissors or pinking shears

Sewing machine with contrasting thread (optional)

There is something so enticing about oilcloth. Perhaps it's the bright colors and retro patterns, or maybe it's the way it wipes clean so easily. Either way, it is a great ingredient for any craft project. These placemats and coasters are super cute and can be made with or without using a sewing machine. The materials below are enough to make a set of four placemats and four coasters. Don't forget to save your leftover scraps to make Wonder Cuffs (page 55) or Oilcloth Flowers (page 69).

1. Trace your shapes with pencil onto the wrong side of the oilcloth and then cut them out. I used vintage serving trays as inspiration for my shapes and included two sets of sample patterns (see Figs. 1 and 2). Use pinking shears or other decorative scissors if a fancy edge is desired.

2. If you don't plan to stitch designs onto the oilcloth, then you are done! Wasn't that easy?

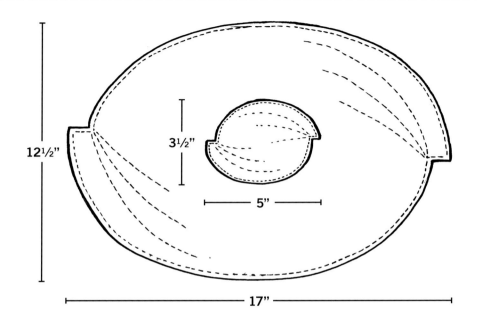

3. If you are doing decorative stitching on the oilcloth, check out Vinyl 101 on page 226 for some helpful tips.

4. Let's stitch! Trace your design with pencil onto the oilcloth (you can erase it when you are done), then carefully stitch along your lines. Refer to the sidebar for help stitching

Here are two tips for making double-sided placemats and coasters:
• Use double-sided tape to stick your two pieces wrong side together before sewing. This will help keep them from sliding apart.
• If you are using pinking shears to make a decorative edge on your double-sided mats, be sure to sew the pieces together before cutting around the edge. This way the edges will match up on your finished product.

2

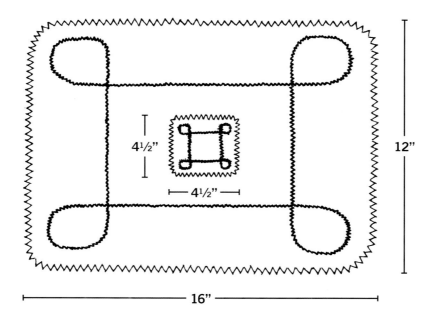

4¹/₂"

├─ 4¹/₂" ─┤

12"

├────────── 16" ──────────┤

the double-sided placemats and coasters. To add rick-rack, place it along your lines and slowly sew over the trim. I have to warn you that sewing rick-rack onto your placemats and coasters is a little time consuming. But if you are a rick-rack fanatic like I am, it will be time well spent when you see how cute it looks!

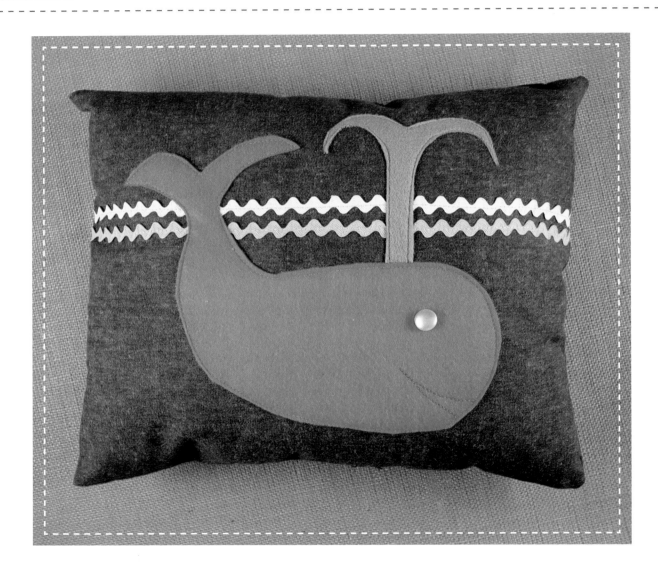

WHALE OF A PILLOW

YOU'LL NEED

One 14-inch by 32-inch piece of denim or other sturdy fabric

2 yards of rick-rack in desired colors (I used two shades of blue)

Two pieces of felt in desired colors

Cardstock or newspaper

Thread in several colors

Poly fiberfill or pillow stuffing

Button

TOOLS

Pencil

Straight pins

Sewing machine (recommended, but you can also sew this project by hand)

Scissors

Measuring tape

Needle

Chopstick or pencil

This cheerful appliquéd whale pillow is a fun one-afternoon project—perfect for the beginner who has mastered straight seams and wants to try out something a bit more challenging. The materials are also remarkably affordable—some felt, a denim remnant, rick-rack, and, of course, a love for whales! Check out Sewing 101 on page 22 if you need help.

1. Pin the first row of rick-rack to the long fabric rectangle in a horizontal line 5 inches from the top, as seen in Fig. 1A. Sew it on using a straight stitch, leaving a short tail of rick-rack hanging off each edge. Repeat with the second piece of rick-rack, positioning it ¾ of an inch below the first one.

2. Use the whale and spout drawings from Fig. 1B to make patterns—you can enlarge them using a copier or just draw them freehand on newspaper in the right size. Pin each pattern to a sheet of felt and cut out each piece.

3. Fold the long rectangle of fabric in half, wrong sides together, so it measures 14 inches tall and 16 inches across. Place the whale and spout in the center of the pillow front, about 4 inches in from the sides and about 3 inches in from the top and bottom. Pin just

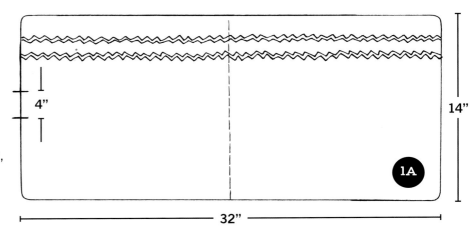

If you want to try other felt projects, how about . . .

"Knit or Die" Patch on page 40

Felt Flowers on page 67

Superhero Slip + Boxers on page 143

Rock + Roll Kitty Toy on page 182

You can also appliqué the whale, or anything else you dream up, on a bag, T-shirt, jacket, or skirt. Felt is perfect to experiment with—it's cheap, so if you hate what you just cut out, no problem. It doesn't need hemming or any other special treatment, so try drawing designs free-hand with a fabric marker, cutting them out, and sewing or gluing them on anything you please.

the spout in place and sew it on, going slowly around the curved edges.

4. Sew the smile on the whale in a contrast thread color, as shown in the diagram. Pin the whale on, covering the base of the spout, and stitch it on.

5. Now fold the fabric in half, right sides together, so the design is on the inside. Pin the three open sides together, matching up the rick-rack as evenly as you can. Leave a 3- to 4-inch space (see Fig. 1A) on the side below the rick-rack rows for turning the pillow right side out and stuffing it.

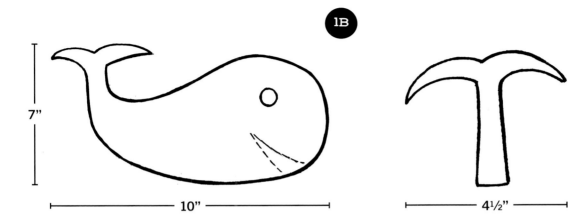

6. Stitch the top and side together with a ½-inch seam allowance, stopping at the space you left open and backstitching to reinforce the seam. Sew the bottom and side seams the same way.

7. Turn the pillow right side out through the opening and use a chopstick or pencil to push the corners out.

8. Stuff the pillow with the fiberfill, using the chopstick to push it into the corners. When it is full, use the invisible stitch to sew up the opening with a needle and thread, adding a bit more fiberfill as you go.

9. Sew a vintage button on for the eye, as shown in the diagram—or, if the pillow is for a small child, sew on a small felt circle instead.

MAGNETS GALORE
+ INSPIRATION BOARD

FOR GRAB-BAG MAGNETS YOU'LL NEED

1/2-inch round magnets

Cookie sheet

Coins, game pieces, buttons, vintage brooches, or other flat-backed objects

Silicone sealer glue

TOOLS

Wire clippers

Toothpicks

FOR MARBLE MAGNETS YOU'LL NEED

Clear flat-backed glass marbles

Art paper, origami paper, pictures, or images of your choice

1/2-inch round magnets

Plain white paper

Cookie sheet

Silicone sealer glue

TOOLS

Sharp scissors

Handmade magnets are a perfect present for holidays, birthdays, or just for yourself. Make a set of magnets topped with glass marbles or assorted small objects to hold everything from the menus and report cards on your refrigerator to the pictures that inspire you on a metal board in your office or work space.

I made this collage after visiting my brother and his family in New York; I used a picture and a few souvenirs and added a fortune and a design for a new handbag with a fabric swatch. I anchored everything with a fun assortment of magnets I made in an hour or two.

Note: For durable magnets, I highly recommend using silicone glue for a clear finish and strong hold. I don't suggest using a hot glue gun for this project—hot glue is very brittle after cooling, and your magnet can pop right off after it sets, which is quite annoying.

GRAB-BAG MAGNETS

1. Place your magnets on a cookie sheet or other metal surface, spacing them out so there's at least an inch between each one.

Look over the objects you plan to attach to make sure the backs are clean, dry, and (relatively) flat. Apply a small glob of the silicone sealer to the center of the back of the first piece and place it on a magnet. Repeat with all other pieces.

2. Allow the glue to set for at least 2 hours before moving the magnets.

MARBLE MAGNETS

1. Sort your glass marbles to make sure they are clear and not badly flawed. Place a marble on your paper or picture to see how it will look in action. When you've chosen images you like, cut out them out in squares or circles that are bigger than the marble itself, so there's excess paper showing on all sides of the glass. Cut a sheet of white paper into inch-wide strips and then cut the strips into approximately 1-inch squares.

2. Apply a glob of silicone sealer to the back of the glass marble and press it down over the image you've chosen. The glue should spread out evenly—if you don't have enough, lift the marble up and add a little more. Apply a little dab of glue to the back of the image and

If you're using coins (see Fig. 1A), remember that they're often magnetic as well—test them before you glue to make sure they'll stay on the way you want them to.

Broken jewelry (see Fig. 1B) is perfect for magnets—just use wire clippers to remove the pinback on a brooch or the clip on an earring. Also test to see if metal jewelry is magnetic.

If you're using buttons (see Fig. 1C), use a toothpick to remove the excess glue that gets pushed up through the holes in the button when you glue it.

Game pieces and tiles also make very cool magnets!

press it down onto a square of white paper. (This second layer helps protect the image from darkening if the magnet shows through.) Repeat to glue all your marbles. (See Fig. 1D.)

3. Let the marbles set for at least an hour or two. When they are completely dry, cut around the marbles, trimming all the excess paper away from the glass pieces with sharp scissors.

4. Arrange your magnets on a cookie sheet or other metal surface, spacing them out so there's at least an inch between each one.

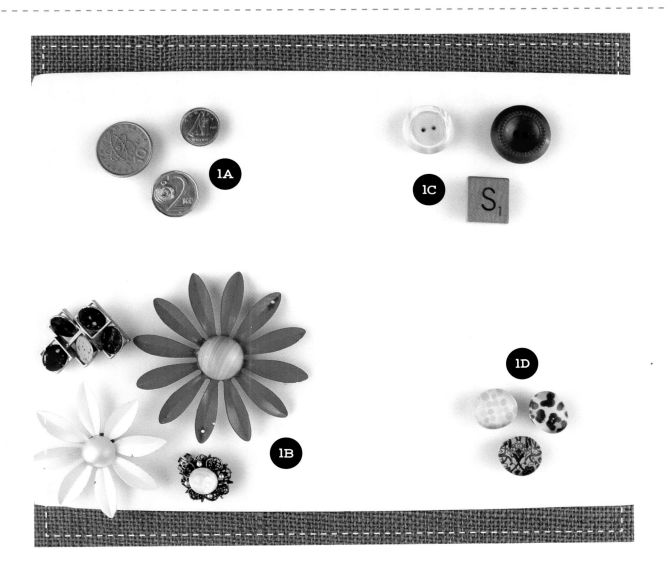

5. Apply a small glob of the silicone sealer to the center of the back of the first marble and place it on a magnet. Repeat with all other pieces. Let them set for at least an hour, preferably two, before moving them.

INSPIRATION BOARD

1. Find a metal sheet to serve as the board. I bought mine at the hardware store for $6 and had it drilled with two holes for hanging it on the wall. I found the smaller piece of metal (shown in the photograph) at a thrift store.

YOU'LL NEED

Metal sheet (For the board in the photograph, I used an 8-inch by 10-inch sheet, but for my studio wall, I used a 4-foot by 5-foot sheet of galvanized steel from the hardware store to display larger pictures and fabrics.)

Pictures, images, letters, to-do lists—anything you want to look at

Magnets

Use your favorite photographs to make unique, personalized marble magnets! Just scan the pictures, crop or resize them to ½ to ¾ inches across, and print them out at home or at a copy shop.

Other instant-gratification projects include Aromatherapy Massage Oil (page 114) and It's Spring! Bike Helmet (page 203).

2. Gather pictures, magazine clippings, or any other visuals that inspire you, like souvenirs from a trip or an event, and arrange them on the board. Use magnets to secure them in an arrangement you like.

3. Change the images as you find new ones or as you finish projects you're working on.

BOUDOIR LAMPSHADE

BY RACHEL

YOU'LL NEED

Newspaper

Old fabric-covered porous lampshade

Acrylic paint

Cup of water

Vintage fabric and/or embroidered tablecloth or napkins

Decoupage medium

TOOLS

Pie tin or paint pallet

Paintbrush (or sponge brush)

Paintbrush (1 to 2 inches wide)

Scissors

I'm not a big fan of plain, old, boring department-store lampshades, and there seems to be no shortage of yellow-stained ones of all sizes at your neighborhood thrift store or weekend garage sale. How about creating a retro-style lampshade to dress up your living space? You can create an adorable lampshade to match your home decor for just a few dollars.

I *am* a big fan of vintage embroidered tablecloths and linens. Even if they're a bit shredded, these beauties are just screaming to be given a new life on your lampshade. Here's how to go to town on this project!

1. Cover a flat surface (table or floor) with newspaper to protect it from spills. Wipe off your lampshade with a damp cloth.

2. Squeeze out a dollop of acrylic paint and pour ¼ cup of water into the pie tin or paint pallet.

3. Mix the water with the acrylic paint to thin out the consistency of your paint.

4. Dip your sponge paintbrush into the paint and begin to sponge the color over the entire surface of the lampshade. To obtain an irregular and textured surface, apply just one layer of paint. For a solid-colored surface, use at least two coats. Feel free to use as many colors as you like. For this project I just used one pink lipstick color for the base color on the shade.

5. Let the lampshade dry for at least 30 minutes.

6. Cut out the flowers and/or embroidered shapes from your tablecloth or napkins. Arrange them over the lampshade until you find a pattern that you like.

7. Use a clean paintbrush to paint a thick layer of decoupage medium on the back of your first cut-out shape and press it firmly onto the lampshade.

You may have figured out by now that I am a huge fan of vintage appliqué. If you are too, use some to make your own Cowgirl Drivin' Machine (page 209). Don't forget: If you have a dog, you can also use appliqué to embellish Rosie's Four-Legged Warmers for your pup (page 187).

8. Paint a layer of decoupage medium over the cut-out shape.

9. Repeat steps 7 and 8 until your design is complete.

10. (optional) If you want to add the base color to your cut-out, simply take your paintbrush and repeat step 3 to sponge color onto your cut-out shapes.

11. Now use an old lamp base or make another trip to the thrift store or garage sale for the perfect base to match your retro lampshade.

MOD SQUARES WALL COLLAGE

YOU'LL NEED

Newspaper or scrap paper

Nine 4-inch by 4-inch canvases

Nine colors of acrylic paint (I used Tangerine, True Orange, Sunkiss Yellow, Green, Dusty Green, Royal Blue, Medium Blue, Holiday Red, and Hot Pink.)

TOOLS

Foam paintbrushes (the more you have, the faster the project goes)

- Paint stripes or geometric shapes for a more mod look.
- Paint the entire batch of canvases the same color or varying shades of the same color(s)—all blues or all greens, for example.
- Glue found objects or photographs to the canvases to create interesting collages.
- If you're in the mood to redecorate, try the Whale of a Pillow (page 91).

It may not earn a spot on the wall at an art museum, but if you have limited drawing abilities (like me!) you can still create your own masterpiece. This is also a great way to add some color to a room without breaking your pocketbook.

1. Put some newspaper or scrap paper down to cover the surface where you will be painting. Be sure to put enough down so that you have a place to set each canvas to dry.

2. Paint each canvas a different color. Rinse paintbrushes and allow brushes and canvases to dry. (Drying time is about an hour.)

3. Repeat step two until you are satisfied with the color saturation on each canvas. Some colors may require more coats of paint than others.

4. Decide how to display your artwork: You could hang all of the canvases in a row, hang them three by three, put a few here and a few there. . . .

BY TORIE

EASY ETCHED GLASS

YOU'LL NEED

Something glass to etch

Newspaper or scrap paper

Contact paper or stickers

Masking tape

Glass etching cream

TOOLS

Scissors

Precision knife and cutting mat or cardboard, if you will be cutting your own designs

Rubber gloves

Paintbrush

Glass etching is a quick and simple way to personalize and spruce up a plain glass object.

1. Clean your glass object and allow it to dry.

2. Place some newspaper or scrap paper down over your working surface. If you will be using a precision knife, put a cutting mat or piece of cardboard down too so you don't cut into your table surface.

3. If you are creating your own design instead of using stickers, cut your design out of contact paper.

4. Stick your design or stickers onto your glass object where you would like them to be. Now mask off any parts of the object that you do not want to etch. Smooth down all of the edges of the contact paper or stickers and tape, so you don't have any cream sneaking underneath them.

5. Put on your rubber gloves. Following the directions on your glass etching cream, apply the cream to the glass using a paintbrush. Allow it to set for the recommended time on the bottle. Then, following the instructions, rinse off the cream.

6. If the glass is etched to your liking, remove the stickers and tape and you're finished! (If the etching cream was not left on long enough to etch the glass, apply more and wait a little longer.)

Always, always, always wear rubber gloves when working with etching cream! If it cuts through glass, you don't want to see what it will do to your skin!

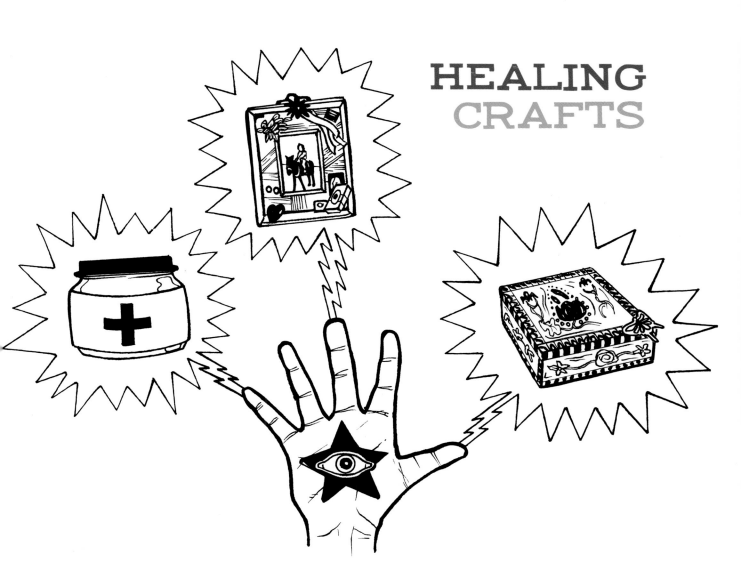

HEALING
CRAFTS

FORGET-ME-NOT SHRINE

BY CATHY

For the last eight years, I've had a box in my closet marked "Dad" that is full of very special junk. When my dad passed away, I went through his belongings and picked out seemingly insignificant but beautiful objects to remember him by: an old velvet flower, an empty lighter, two tokens from Treasure Island in Florida, a souvenir tape measure, a penny with the Lord's Prayer pressed into it. Then there were the significant and emotional objects: the gold pen engraved with his name, a stack of old IBM punch cards that he carried around and wrote on, a kindergarten portrait of me that he kept, the three packs of cigarettes he had in his pocket when he died. I knew that someday these objects would come together to become an incredible work of art that would forever represent my dad and all that I felt about him. This is that work of art.

There are no specific instructions for this project. Each shrine will contain a unique array of objects, and the process is a personal one that you have to work through on your own. It can be quite hard, but I highly recommend it as part of the healing process.

Here are some tips that may help you in assembling your shrine.

1. Start with a box. It gives your piece dimension, and the inside bottom and outside top can work as shelves on which you can glue larger objects.

2. Consider enlarging copies of original photos. This way you can choose the image size and don't have to give up your only original.

3. Use decoupage medium to adhere paper items and hot glue to affix larger, unusually shaped objects.

4. Use paper items—like letters, newspaper clippings, and book pages—for a backdrop to line the inside of your box.

5. Include simple, everyday objects.

6. I chose to use a combination of objects that had positive emotions attached to them. You'll want to create a work that you can hang on your wall and look at every day without feeling incredibly sad.

SOOTHING SALVES

BY SUSAN

YOU'LL NEED

1/3 cup beeswax

Small jars or tins

2/3 cup olive oil

1/3 cup sweet almond oil

10 drops vitamin E oil (optional)

Essential oils:

10–15 drops rosemary

20 drops peppermint

20 drops lavender

20 drops calendula

20 drops comfrey

Stickers, art paper, or labels

Glue stick

Water-based sealant

TOOLS

Large, flat saucepan

2–4 cup Pyrex measuring cup

Chopstick or metal spoon

Cookie sheet

Dropper

You can make your own salves using herbal additives and essential oils that promote healing. If you like, you can melt the salve in a Crockpot™ instead of on the stove.

Two quick warnings: First, make sure your measuring cup is Pyrex, not untreated glass, and second, if you are pregnant (or making salve for a pregnant woman), leave out the rosemary essential oil, as it can be harmful during pregnancy.

1. Place the Pyrex measuring cup in the saucepan. Add enough water to the pan so that the cup sits in several inches of water. Bring the water to a boil. Put beeswax in the cup and stir occasionally with the chopstick or metal spoon as it melts. Meanwhile, arrange the tins or jars on a cookie sheet or other flat surface, leaving a little space between the containers for easy pouring. As the water in the pan evaporates, add more to make sure it doesn't boil dry.

SOOTHING SALVE +
AROMATHERAPY MASSAGE OIL

2. Add the olive and sweet almond oils and continue to stir. (Adding room-temperature oil will cause the beeswax to solidify again, but it won't take as long to melt this time.)

3. Once the mixture has melted completely, begin adding essential oils with a dropper, continuing to stir. Adjust the ratio to your liking. Add the vitamin E oil (if you're using it).

4. Slowly pour the salve into the containers, leaving a little room at the top of each one. (If one overfills, carefully spoon some off before it cools and put the extra into another container.) As you start running out of the salve, check to see if any containers need topping off.

5. Let the salves cool on a counter (or in the refrigerator for a quicker cool) and let stand undisturbed until they are room temperature.

6. Decorate the jars or tins with stickers, art paper, or labels. For each of my labels, I cut a 1-inch by 3-inch piece of white paper and used a glue stick to apply it to the jar. Then I cut two thin strips of red paper and crossed them at right angles, used a glue stick to add them on, and covered the entire design with a coat of water-based sealant.

To infuse your own calendula and comfrey oils, just combine 1 cup of olive oil (or a mix of olive and sweet almond oils) with ½ ounce of calendula and ½ ounce of comfrey, both available in bulk at health food stores. Infuse the mixture in a Crockpot on low for 3–4 hours, strain it, and retain the oil, discarding the solids. (You can also infuse the herbs in oil in a Pyrex cup in a saucepan of boiling water, or in a double boiler, for 45 minutes to an hour.) Use this oil in the salve recipe instead of plain olive oil and omit the calendula and comfrey essential oils, but use the normal amounts of rosemary, peppermint, and lavender.

See more packaging and labeling ideas on page 260.

AROMATHERAPY MASSAGE OIL

YOU'LL NEED

Sweet almond oil

Essential oils

Bottles or jars

Paper and glue stick or stickers, plus water-based sealant, for labeling

TOOLS

Glass or Pyrex measuring cup with a lip for pouring

Dropper

This is a true instant-gratification project! In under a minute, you can create a custom-blended massage oil to help you energize or relax. There are hundreds of essential oils to try—I've suggested a few combinations I like, but you can create your own unique blends. *Note:* Rosemary essential oil should not be used by pregnant women.

1. Pour the sweet almond oil into the measuring cup.

2. Add the essential oils, one at a time if using more than one. Adjust the ratio to your liking—if the massage oil is too strongly scented, just add more sweet almond oil.

3. Pour the mixture into bottles and label. For the cobalt blue bottle, I used a simple origami paper label affixed with a glue stick and covered it with a coat of water-based sealant.

Use 8–15 drops of essential oil(s) per ounce of sweet almond oil, depending on your preference. Some essential oils (like peppermint and rosemary) are stronger in a blend; others (lavender, for example) are much more subtle.

For an instant mini-aromatherapy treatment, massage a few drops of your blend at your temples, wrists, and neck.

FOR RELAXING:
2 parts lavender
1 part ylang-ylang

FOR SOOTHING:
2 parts lavender
1 part sandalwood
1 part chamomile

FOR HEADACHES:
1 part lavender
1 part peppermint

Massage gently into temples, on the back of the neck, and along your jaw line.

FOR SLEEPLESSNESS:
2 parts lavender
1 part chamomile
1 part tangerine

FOR ENERGY:
3 parts peppermint
1 part rosemary

FOR JET LAG:
2 parts lavender
2 parts peppermint
1 part rosemary

FOR SORE MUSCLES:
2 parts lavender
1 part rosemary
1 part peppermint
1 part ginger

TIPS

LOVE SPELL MOJO BOX

BY RACHEL

YOU'LL NEED

A vintage wooden box

Paper

Honey (yes, real honey!)

Newspaper

Acrylic paint

Shrink plastic

Permanent markers

Craft glue

Vintage or new pictures

Glitter

Small glass tiles

Vintage buttons

Vintage dice

TOOLS

Pen

Small paintbrush

Do you feel lovesick? Does your heart reach explosive levels of activity when you are in the presence of your secret boyfriend or girlfriend? Will they ever realize how insanely cool you are and how much fun you could have together sneaking Thai food into the movie theater on your third date? A mojo, a magic charm or spell, could do the trick. Conjure love energy by creating a mojo box to contain all of your secret daydreams—and just maybe they will come true!

1. Go to your local thrift or antique store and search for a small vintage wooden box, buttons, pictures, and dice.

2. Think about your secret boyfriend or girlfriend while you write a short love letter. Put a small drop of honey next to your signature. Place your love letter someplace where you can see it while you are working on your Love Spell Mojo Box.

3. Cover a table with newspaper and spread out all of your supplies.

4. Choose acrylic paint color(s) for the outside of your box that represent your secret crush and paint the outside of your box. Let dry for 30 minutes. Choose acrylic paint color(s) that represent you and paint the inside of your box, sprinkling glitter as needed. Let dry 30 minutes.

5. Trace or draw images with permanent markers on your shrink plastic to represent how you would feel to be with your secret crush on a first date. I chose to draw an anatomical image of a heart and some cool flying pirate girls. Follow directions on page 160 to complete your shrink art.

6. Arrange and glue the shrink art images along with tiles, vintage buttons, or other objects of your choice to complete the outside of the box. Let everything dry for two hours.

7. Choose objects that represent your desire to be with your secret crush and how you feel

THE WONDERFUL WORLD OF MOJOS: MORE IDEAS ON MOJO MAKING

How about creating a portable mojo? You can use a matchbox, a small tin box, or a film container to create a mini pocket mojo. If you have a loved one who is ill or just going through a hard time, you can create a personalized mojo to bring them health and good luck. In your mojo note you can describe the meaning of each object you included. Portable mojos also make great gifts!

inside when you see him or her. Arrange and glue these objects inside the box.

8. Take your love note, fold it up, and place it inside your box.

9. When you go to sleep, place your box either next to you on your nightstand or under your pillow.

10. Sweet dreams . . . who knows what will happen tomorrow.

EMERGENCY CRAFT KIT— CRAFTS TO THE RESCUE!

BY RACHEL

YOU'LL NEED

Secondhand or new makeup bag

Newspaper

Small tubes of fabric or acrylic paint

Craft glue

Round mini mirrors or other durable objects

Trim (rick-rack, ball fringe, or ribbon)

Glitter (optional)

TOOLS

Small paintbrush

SMALL ARTS AND CRAFTS SUPPLIES

Feathers

Mini tarot card set

Elvis matches

Lollipop

Oil pastels

Small squares of paper

Fabric wings

Pipe cleaners

Needle and thread

Felt

Did you break up with your extra-special friend today? Did they finally track you down for jury duty? Are you traumatized by your upcoming 10-hour plane trip to visit your in-laws for the holidays? What can you do to ease the pain of life's small, medium, and large disasters? You desperately need an **Emergency Craft Kit.**

1. Buy a new or secondhand makeup bag—I like a boxlike design. Makeup bags are perfect because they usually contain ideal craft compartments normally used for eye pencils, lipsticks, and small grooming tools.

2. Cover a table with newspaper.

3. Paint the inside and outside of your bag in bright colors using either fabric paint or acrylic paint. Let dry for 2 hours or until dry to the touch.

4. Glue mini mirrors or any other durable objects to create a design on the outside of

your bag. Finish off your design with the trim of your choice.

5. Paint the inside of your box with a bright color and cover with glitter as desired. Let dry for 2 hours.

6. Gather small arts and craft supplies of your choice and fill up your bag!

Use your Emergency Craft Kit to promote change, as well. Art supplies can come in handy when you find yourself at a political rally or an event for social change. Create a sign or poster or design a shirt on the spot with supplies from your Emergency Craft Kit. Don't leave home without it!

7. Keep your Emergency Craft Kit handy at all times and use as directed. Use your kit for 1 hour, up to four times a day, to relieve any of the following symptoms: lovesickness, homesickness, boredom, fear of flying, fear of relatives, housebound and slightly stir crazy feeling, or rainy day blues. Use until symptoms decrease. The Emergency Craft Kit is officially approved for use by Super Crafty, LLC.

HOLY
SCRAP

TRIBUTE CANDLE

YOU'LL NEED

Blank glass inspirational candle

Foil or decorative paper for background

Photo of your favorite icon or loved one

Decoupage medium

Craft glue

Decorative accents like sewing trim and plastic charms

TOOLS

Scissors or pinking shears

Paintbrush

Please remember to consider fire safety when gluing decorations to your candle. Don't glue anything near the flame and never leave a burning candle unattended!

Blank inspirational candles are available at grocery stores or specialty markets. You can also look at thrift stores for something similar.

1. Cut a shape out of paper or foil for your background. Size it according to the dimensions of your candle. Use pinking shears to add a decorative edge. Ovals or rectangles look great.

2. Cut out your picture so that when it is glued onto the decorative shape the background will frame your picture nicely.

3. Use decoupage medium to affix the picture onto the backdrop. When it is dry, use craft glue to attach the entire thing onto the glass. Decoupage medium works best when gluing two porous items together (like paper). Craft glue works best when gluing onto a nonporous surface (like glass).

4. Use craft glue to add the decorative accents around the picture. I used rick-rack trim to encircle my image then added some plastic flowers and a velvet leaf to the bottom. You can find objects like this at craft stores or estate sales.

WINGED POCKET SHRINE

BY RACHEL

YOU'LL NEED

Small vintage coin purse

Acrylic or fabric paint

Colored paper (or ready-made paper flowers)

Decoupage medium

Craft glue

Glitter

Fabric wings

Rhinestones

Vintage metal stamping or piece of jewelry

Vintage plastic flower

TOOLS

Paintbrush

Scissors

If you are planning a trip, you may need more than your travel toothbrush, handy wipes, and donut neck pillow. How do you ward off flat tires, tailgaters, turbulence, screaming and drooling babies right smack next to your precious window seat, and the aftermath of drive-thru food? You desperately need a Winged Pocket Shrine to help you create a happy protective bubble that won't burst under any condition until you arrive at your final destination. Your portable shrine will end up on your future travel supply lists.

1. Find a vintage fabric coin purse.

2. Paint the outside of your purse with acrylic or fabric paint as desired. Let dry for 30 minutes. Paint the inside of your coin purse as desired and let dry for 30 minutes.

3. Cut flowers from paper to design the outside of your coin purse. You can also use ready-made paper flowers from your local craft or scrapbook store. Arrange your flowers on the outside of your purse, glue in place, and paint a layer of decoupage medium to seal your design.

4. Sprinkle glitter over the outside of the purse before the decoupage medium dries.

5. Paint your wings with fabric or acrylic paint and let them dry for 1 hour. Glue rhinestones on your wings for added sparkle and positive energy. Glue wings on each side of the coin purse with craft glue. Let dry for 2 hours.

6. Glue rhinestones as desired on the outside of your coin purse.

7. Choose a vintage metal stamping or piece of jewelry that represents good luck to keep inside your Winged Pocket Shrine.

8. Paint your metal stamping with acrylic paint as desired and embellish with vintage flowers and rhinestones.

9. Pack your Winged Pocket Shrine for your next travel adventure!

You can make your own miniwings from shrink art by visiting our clip art on page 162, enlarging the set of wings, and following the shrink art directions on page 160.

To make your own fabric wings, all you need is a half a yard of fabric, felt, needle and thread, and scissors. Enlarge our clip art wings to your desired size and use them as a pattern to cut out two sets of fabric wings and two sets of felt wings. Place the felt pieces in between your fabric layers and glue or sew them together—the felt will add some body to your wings, and you can use a needle and thread to sew defined lines into your wings.

You can also troll your local craft store for ready-made wings.

BLOSSOM FERTILITY SHRINE

BY RACHEL

YOU'LL NEED

Wooden box

Acrylic paint

Craft glue

Vintage photograph

Vintage velvet flower

Vintage trim

Glitter

Large pod or other meaningful object

Decoupage medium

TOOLS

Paintbrush

Paper

Pen

Do you get a funny feeling in your womb area when you catch a glimpse of tiny hands grasping onto a well-loved stuffed bunny? Do you find yourself staring at the baby in front of you in the grocery line, and get caught by her mom who wonders if you're some crazy stalker? Do you linger at the rack of miniature clothes in the thrift store? These may all be signs that you are ready to reproduce. Not to get all metaphysical with you, but it is damn important that your mind and body are in agreement and ready to rock and roll in the reproduction process. A fertility shrine may be just what you need to give a little boost to successful baby making.

1. Spend some time in your local thrift, antique, or craft stores browsing for objects that represent aspects of the reproduction process.

2. Gather objects and decide what each one represents to you. It is vital to personalize this process so that you create a powerful shrine to

inspire you as you venture into this huge step in your life.

3. Find a vintage or new wooden box to use as the container for all your objects.

4. Using acrylic paints, decorate the inside and outside of your box to represent your ideas about having a baby. Let your box dry for 30 minutes.

5. Arrange your objects inside the box as desired. Think about how the objects can be arranged to reveal a story that will inspire you.

Create a Tribute Candle (page 125) to accompany your fertility shrine for maximum juju energy!

6. Glue objects into the box. Decorate the shrine with glitter, fabric flowers, trims, and other beautiful things.

7. I added the pod to send good baby-making energy to my womb. I found the pod at a random estate sale, but I would suggest going for a nature walk and looking for pods, searching your local craft store, or seeing what you can dig up in your backyard.

8. Write down what each object means on a small piece of paper and glue to the back of your shrine with decoupage medium.

9. Take care of your mind and body and remember to have fun baby making!

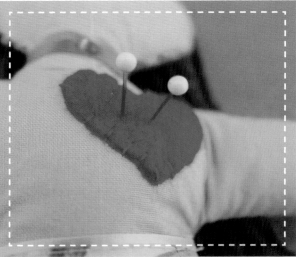

HAPPY HEX VOODOO DOLL

BY TORIE

YOU'LL NEED

1/4 yard fabric, or large enough fabric scraps to cut out two doll shapes

Fusible interfacing

3-inch by 4-inch piece of fabric to cover the back of the head (if desired)

Craft glue

1-inch piece of red felt (or desired color for heart)

Yarn (whatever color you desire for the hair of your doll)

Polyfill or pillow stuffing

5-inch square of oilcloth or fabric of choice

1-inch piece of pink felt (or desired color for pocket)

Fabric glue

20 inches of ribbon (to attach the apron)

3-1/2 inches of ribbon (for necklace)

One rhinestone

TOOLS

Scissors

Iron

Straight pins

Sewing thread and needles

Sewing machine (recommended)

Clear or masking tape

Pinking shears

J ust saying the words "voodoo doll" is enough to scare some people out of their wits, but what many people don't know is that voodoo is often used for good—love spells, healing—and not just for black magic. It's up to you how you plan on using your voodoo doll! Just remember the karmic rule—what you do to someone else comes back to you, only three times worse.

1. Cut two of the doll shapes in Fig. 1 out of your chosen fabric for the body of the doll. Also cut two doll shapes out of fusible interfacing.

2. Iron the doll cut-outs to remove any wrinkles. Then fuse the interfacing to each piece, following the manufacturer's directions.

3. Cut your 3-inch by 4-inch piece of fabric to fit the back of the doll's head. Glue or pin it onto the right side of the piece that will be the back of the doll. Starting in the center, stitch around and around to make a spiral that will end on the perimeter of the doll's head. (The spiral stitching is optional. If you like, just stitch around the perimeter of the doll's head to hold this piece of fabric in place).

4. Cut a small heart out of red felt. Glue or pin the heart where you'd like it on the piece of the doll that will be its front. Sew the heart on, either by hand or using the appliqué or zig-zag stitch on your sewing machine.

5. Cut 30 6-inch pieces of yarn (or more if you want your doll to have more hair).

6. Take one of the two doll cut-outs and half of the yarn and line up the ends of the yarn along the top of the head on the right side of the fabric. Place a piece of tape across the yarn about ½ inch from the top to hold it in place. Straight stitch along the top of the head (about ¼ inch down) until all of the yarn is secure. Remove the tape.

7. Repeat step 6 with the other doll cut-out and the second half of your cut yarn.

8. With right sides together, pin your two doll pieces. Make sure the hair will stay out of the way when you sew. (I wrapped some tape around the yarn on both pieces about halfway down to hold it all together.)

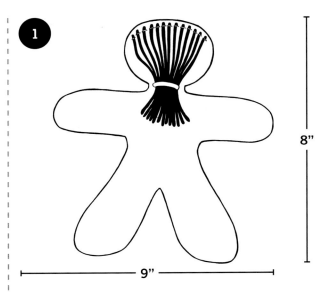

9. Stitch along the perimeter of your doll with a ⅛-inch seam allowance, leaving a 3- to 4-inch opening along one leg. (The larger the opening, the easier it will be to turn your doll right side out and stuff it.)

10. Turn the doll right side out and press out any wrinkles.

11. Take small pieces of batting and stuff your doll to desired fullness. Once full, pin the opening together and use the invisible stitch to sew it closed.

12. Trim the doll's hair to the desired length. You could cut some of the hair into bangs, or leave it all long.

13. To make the apron, cut your oilcloth (or other chosen fabric) into a trapezoid. The one shown here is 2 inches across the top and almost 4 inches across the bottom. Pink around the edges, if desired.

14. Cut a 1-inch-square pocket for the apron out of pink felt (or the color you chose). Pin or glue it to the apron and straight stitch around three sides, leaving the top open. The little apron pocket is intended for you to hold an object (like a strand of hair, for example) from the person you are going to do the voodoo on.

15. Take your 20-inch piece of ribbon and glue or pin it onto the top of the apron. Straight stitch along the top and the bottom of the ribbon to attach it to the apron. Tie the apron to the doll.

16. To make a necklace, glue one end of the shorter piece of ribbon to the back of your doll's neck, in the center. Wrap the ribbon around the neck and glue the other end on top of the first end. Then glue the rhinestone onto the middle of the front of the ribbon necklace.

17. Stick three straight pins in the doll (if desired).

To concoct a love spell, pair the voodoo doll up with the Love Spell Mojo Box (page 117), or if you just like to make dolls, try the Super Sock Monkeys (page 27).

CHURCH OF CRAFT

BY SUSAN

Torie and I are devoted members of Portland Church of Craft, which meets at Rimsky-Korsakoffee House for three hours every month on Sunday afternoons. During our meetings we knit, collage, make jewelry, trade art supplies, or take a class taught by one of the members. We chat about new projects and exchange advice on yarn stores over coffee and dessert. I've had so much fun teaching classes and helping organize meetings with Diane Gilleland, leader of the Portland chapter.

I asked Sister Diane both about her own experiences with spiritual creativity and how to start your own chapter of Church of Craft if your community doesn't already have one.

HOW DID YOU GET STARTED WITH CHURCH OF CRAFT?

While I was living in the Bay Area, a group of my friends decided to get together for an "arts and crafts day." We had so much fun, we started meeting monthly and playing with all kinds of beads, yarn, glue guns, glitter, and the like.

Over time, I realized that these meetings held much more value than just fun. When we were all in the throes of creating, our conversations deepened very naturally. The group had a unique and very positive energy, which I believe was fostered by our joy in the crafting. After our group had been meeting for just a short time, we all began making huge changes for the better in our individual lives—leaving stale jobs and relationships, moving to new places, taking up new studies. I believe it was the renewing influence of these crafting sessions that helped move us in these directions.

When I returned to Portland (my own huge change), I wanted to re-create that group energy and explore bringing it to a larger community. I happened to read about Church of Craft in *BUST* [magazine], and just loved the concept—spirituality through creativity!

HOW DOES SOMEONE START A NEW CHAPTER IN THEIR COMMUNITY?

Go to **www.churchofcraft.org** and send an email to Callie Janoff, the co-founder of the group. She's a very busy person and receives a lot of requests to start chapters, so if you don't get a response to your first email, persevere! You might try sending an email to the flock leader in the city nearest yours and ask for help. I contacted Betsey Brock, who runs the Seattle Church of Craft; she was tremendously supportive and got Callie to respond to me. They both provided me with lots of encouragement.

Because you need to be a minister to start a group, you'd then need to go to the Universal Life Church website, **www.ulc.org**, and get an online ordination. They will ordain you at no charge, and the process takes about five minutes. [*Author's* *note:* Your state's legal requirements for performing ministerial duties may be different.]

Then, find a meeting space. It might be a private home, a local coffeehouse, or a park. Just make sure it's easy to get to via car and public transportation and that you have the owner's permission to meet there. Publicize your meeting by telling everyone you know and placing announcements on as many community websites as you can find. You can also make flyers and post them in places haunted by creative people.

Once you have a few meetings under your belt, and you're sure you want to make this commitment, check back in with Callie. Either she or a flock leader in a nearby city will interview you briefly, to make sure your intentions for your new flock are aligned with the Church of Craft mission. After that interview, you can have your own little ordination ceremony and be considered a full minister in the Church of Craft.

WHAT MAKES CHURCH OF CRAFT A CHURCH?

If you set aside the teachings and trappings of organized religion, then what you're left with is the essence of a church. It's a safe space where people congregate to renew their spirits and connect meaningfully with one another. And this is exactly what Church of Craft is—a safe space for people to renew themselves and connect through creative play. Crafting is wonderful because it's universally accessible!

WHAT ARE MEETINGS LIKE?

First and foremost, I love to see people interacting at our meetings. Crafting is such a natural common ground, and I find that when people are making things, they are happy and excited, and their shyness tends to drop away. At our meetings, I usually hear conversations about big themes—life and love and meaning—with very little stale "what-do-you-do-for-a-living" talk. I think people absolutely crave deeper connection with each other, but it's very difficult to find that depth in the usual social situations. Crafting is a wonderful bridge to great conversations.

I am always happy to see people coming to our meetings by themselves. This indicates that they feel safe in the environment and embraced by the group. I know how hard it can be to walk into a room full of strangers all by yourself. I'm proud that our meetings provide such a welcoming environment.

Second, there's a lot of valuable exchange at our meetings. I always see folks giving each other the address of a wonderful new yarn store, or an online source for jewelry components, or a contact for an upcoming craft bazaar. I see people making plans to get together later to teach each other to knit. I see books and patterns change hands. Our members seem to love sharing their resources with one another, and I believe that openness is driven by the joy they feel in the creative state.

WARDROBE REVOLUTION

SULTRY SLIP

BY SUSAN

YOU'LL NEED

Flower-shape patterns

Felt in desired colors (I used three colors—red, dark red, and dark green)

Slip

Seed beads in desired color

3 yards lace (for this slip, I used 2-2/3 yards of 1-inch-wide red lace)

TOOLS

Scissors

Straight pins

Needle and thread

Sewing machine (recommended for attaching lace)

Boring beige and white slips crowd the racks at thrift stores and department stores alike. Fancy up a plain slip for a sultry custom nightgown or little cocktail dress.

1. Using the patterns on page 67, cut flower shapes of your choice in several sizes out of two felt colors. Layer them and pin them to the slip in the desired patterns. I sewed two flowers to the front of my slip, but you could certainly add many more!

2. Using a needle and complementary thread color, hand-sew the flowers onto the slip, using small stitches spaced about ¼ inch apart. Stitch around the perimeter of each flower layer and around the center circle.

3. Cut leaf shapes out of your third color (using the pattern on page 150) and sew them on in the same way.

4. Hand-stitch seed beads to the bodice of the slip, spacing them about ½ inch apart. Use tiny stitches to secure the beads, and larger

Other girly projects you might enjoy are Pretty Paper Jewelry (page 81) and Pinup Girl Mermaid Shoe Clips (page 169).

Liven up your wardrobe with charming little accents—like the Super Cool Appliqués (page 39), Granny Chic Sweater Clips (page 79), and the Charming Cloche (see Four-Project Sweater, page 149).

stitches on the inside of the slip between each bead. Knot the thread securely at the end.

5. Use straight pins to secure a row of lace around the bottom of the slip's hem, overlapping the edges slightly at one side seam. Sew the lace on with a medium-length straight stitch on your sewing machine, or by hand, backstitching where the lace meets. Sew on a second row of lace 1½ inches above the first one, if you like.

SUPERHERO SLIP + BOXERS

BY SUSAN

YOU'LL NEED

Embroidery thread, needle, and 7-inch hoop

Felt in desired colors

Boxer shorts

Slip

3 to 4 yards 3/8-inch-wide ribbon (for this slip, I used 3-1/4 yards of blue grosgrain)

TOOLS

Washable fabric marker

Scissors

Straight pins

Sewing machine (recommended)

Measuring tape

This matching set transforms you and a sidekick into nighttime superheroes! All you need is a pair of boxers, a vintage or new thrift store slip, felt, and ribbon—and you'll be fighting crime in no time.

SUPERHERO BOXERS

1. Start the POW! star by first embroidering the letters. This design uses two different stitches, the satin stitch and chain stitch, to form the letters. (Refer to Embroidery 101 on page 274 for help with these.) Place the 7-inch hoop on a larger piece of felt. The pattern for embroidering "POW!" is outlined in Fig. 1A. Copy the letters by hand on your felt using a washable fabric marker—I handwrote mine in capitals as shown, but feel free to design them (or any other slogan) in your own style. Thread an embroidery needle with two 36-inch strands of

thread, doubling it and knotting it at the end so you are sewing with an 18-inch length.

2. Starting with the "P," use a satin stitch to create the left side of the letters and a chain stitch to make the right sides (see Fig. 1B).

3. Stitch an asterisk to finish the exclamation point (pattern also on page 276). Embroider an "!" on another piece of felt for the second star.

4. Cut the stars (in Fig. 2A) out of felt—one

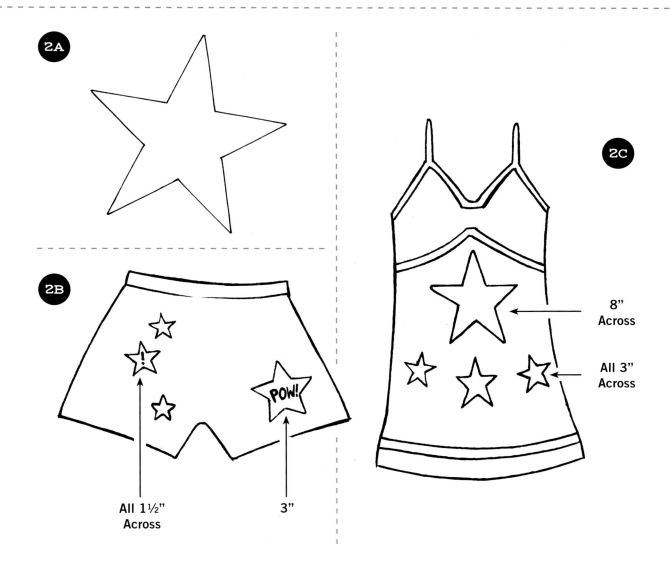

> If you don't want to use a sewing machine, you can hand-stitch the stars on using small stitches about ¼ inch apart. You may want to scale back the amount of ribbon you hand-sew onto a slip . . . it's time-consuming! Try edging just the hem, or just the bodice, for a quicker project.
>
> Other fun appliqué projects include the Sultry Slip (page 141), One-Afternoon Skirt (page 35), and the Knit-It! Bag (page 43).

3 inches across and three that are 1½ inches across. You can enlarge the star pattern on a copier, cut newspaper patterns, and pin them to the felt, or cut them out freehand. Cut the larger star out around the "POW!" and center the "!" on one of the three smaller ones. Remove all traces of the fabric marker with a few drops of water and let dry.

5. Pin the stars to the boxer shorts as shown in Fig. 2B.

6. Sew them on with a medium-length straight stitch close to the edge of the stars.

7. Fight crime!

SUPERHERO SLIP

1. Pin the ribbon around the bodice, neckline, and hem of your slip, as shown in Fig. 2B. Measure the straps of the slip at the point where it fits you well and cut them off. Pin on pieces of ribbon in the same length at front and back and secure with a few stitches.

2. Stitch the ribbon on the slip using a medium-length straight stitch—sew along the upper side first, and along the lower side second, removing pins as you sew. Stitch the ribbon straps on securely, backstitching a few times to hold the seam.

3. Cut out the felt star shapes (as shown in Fig. 2C) in two sizes—one 8 inches across and three that are 3 inches across. You can use the star pattern in Fig. 2A as instructed in the boxers project, or cut them freehand. Pin them to the slip in the pattern shown.

4. Stitch the stars on with a medium-length straight stitch near the perimeter of the stars. Save the world from mass production!

FOUR-PROJECT SWEATER

BY SUSAN

YOU'LL NEED

Old sweater

TOOLS

Scissors

Pinking shears

Straight pins

Needle and thread

Sewing machine

Plus . . .

I created four fresh new pieces out of one tired old $2 acrylic cardigan from the thrift store, all in one afternoon. If your wardrobe needs a style infusion as it's starting to get cold out, look no further than an ancient sweater, a sharp pair of scissors, and a few easy steps for crafty alchemy!

For sewing these projects, I used a zig-zag stitch on a sewing machine. A serger also would be ideal, if you have one. Knits like sweater fabric are best sewn with a ball-point needle, too.

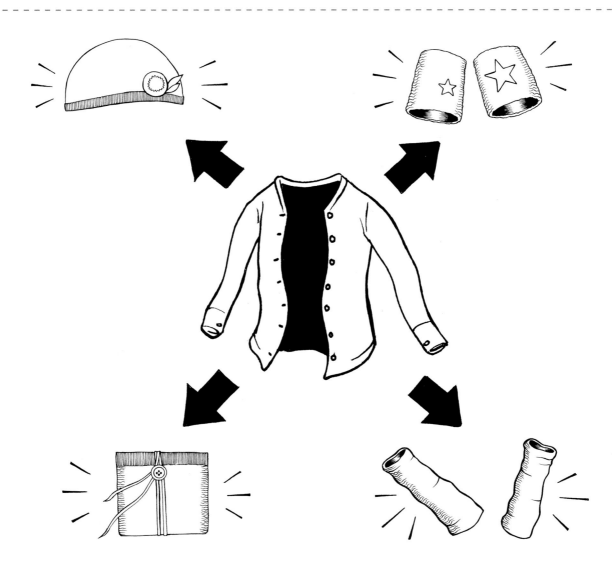

CHARMING CLOCHE

1. Using the guidelines in Fig. 1A, cut out two same-size half-circles from the back of the sweater above the finished ribbed edge.

2. Cut the flower and leaf shapes from Fig. 1B out in felt, using pinking shears to cut out the small flower round. Pin them onto one of the half-circles (which will become the front of the hat)

YOU WILL ALSO NEED

Felt in three colors

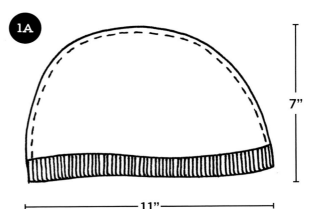

1A

7"

11"

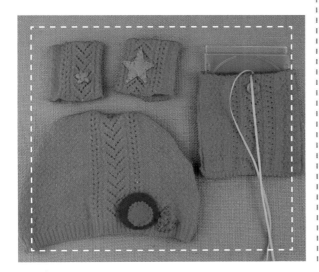

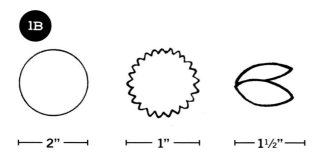

├── 2" ──┤   ├── 1" ──┤   ├── 1½" ──┤

as shown and hand-sew them on, using tiny stitches spaced about ½ inch apart. Tie a secure knot at the end of your sewing.

3. Pin the two halves together, right sides in. Using a sewing machine set on a zig-zag stitch, stitch close to the edge around the curve of the circle, back-stitching at the beginning and end of the seam.

4. Turn the hat right side out and put it on! You look very cute.

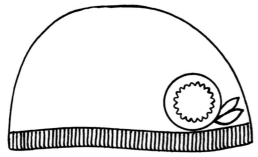

TWO-MINUTE LEGWARMERS

1. Cut the sweater sleeves off at the shoulder seam. This will create very cool modern boot-cut legwarmers. If you like, finish the raw edge with a zig–zag stitch all the way around on each legwarmer.

2. Go out dancing immediately!

POW! WRISTBANDS ②

1. Cut two 4-inch by 7-inch rectangles out of the upper back of the sweater.

2. Cut two stars out of felt and pin them onto the rectangles as in Fig. 2. Attach each star, hand-sewing tiny stitches spaced about ¼ inch apart. Tie a secure knot at the end of your sewing.

YOU WILL ALSO NEED

Felt

3. Using the zig-zag stitch (or serger) described in step 3 of the Charming Cloche pattern, stitch along the edges to finish the long sides of the rectangle so they don't fray.

4. With right sides together, pin each wristband together so the short sides meet. Sew them together with the zig-zag stitch, backstitching at the beginning and end of the seam to hold it tight. Turn them right side out.

5. Slip them on to stay warm while you battle the forces of evil!

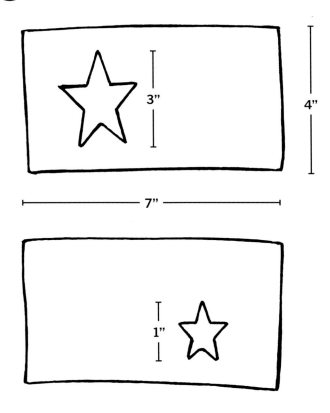

CD COZY

1. Cut out two squares slightly bigger than a CD case (an average size is 5½ inches by 6 inches). If possible, use pieces with one finished ribbed edge from the hem of the sweater. If not, finish one edge on each square with a zig-zag stitch. This will be the top edge.

YOU WILL ALSO NEED:

Two vintage buttons

Ribbon (I used 4 feet of 1/8-inch-wide blue satin ribbon)

2. Line up the squares and stitch around three sides of them using the zig-zag stitch described in step 3 of the Charming Cloche pattern. Backstitch at the beginning and the end to hold the seam securely. Turn the cozy inside out so the seams are inside.

3. Sew on the buttons, centering them in the middle about an inch down from the top of the open side.

4. Fold the ribbon in half and sew it on above the button on one side. To close the cozy, wrap

If you like secondhand crafting, there's a whole chapter devoted to it—Reduce, Reuse, Re-sparkle, which starts on page 243. Reuse glass jars, soda cans, paper towel rolls . . . we have tons of ideas.

the ribbon over the top, around the entire cozy, back over the top, and then wind it around the other button.

5. Start burning mix CDs for holiday presents!

GOTH GIRL CHOKER + ROCKABILLY DOMINO BELT BRACELET

FOR THE CHOKER YOU'LL NEED

Vintage belt

Fancy trim

Strong glue

1 yard of satin cord

Vintage buttons or plastic flowers

14 bead caps

Seven beads

Jewelry eye pins

Acrylic paint or permanent marker (optional)

Vintage or new beads

FOR THE BRACELET YOU'LL NEED

Leftover belt segment

Mini domino (or vintage game piece)

Plastic flowers or vintage buttons

Mini ball fringe (or vintage trim of your choice)

1/2 yard black satin cord

TOOLS

Fabric measuring tape

Scissors

Needle and thread

Hole punch (smaller than the circumference of your grommets)

Mini grommet plier kit

Wire cutter

Round-nose pliers

You know those little vintage belts that appear to be made for your five-year-old cousin rather than for real women? Yes, you know, those cute fabric-covered belts that hang aimlessly from hook after hook in your local thrift store. Now that we have established that these belts cannot possibly serve their original intended purpose, they must be destroyed! Well—not exactly destroyed, *transformed* to adorn other parts of our bodies. Decorate your neck with this fun and liberating project.

GOTH GIRL CHOKER

1. Measure your neck and subtract 2 inches from your number. (These 2 inches will provide the space you need to create a lace-up back for your choker.) For example, if your neck is 14 inches around, then 12 inches will be your key measurement for this project.

2. Cut out a segment from your belt the length of your key measurement.

GOTH GIRL CHOKER

ROCKABILLY DOMINO BELT BRACELET

3. Cut two strips of trim the same length as your belt segment.

4. Sew or glue the trim along the back length of the top and bottom of the belt segment.

5. With your hole punch, punch two or three holes in a row about ¼ inch in from each end of the belt segment.

6. Attach your grommets in each hole.

7. Lace the satin cord back and forth through each set of grommets (like you would lace up your shoes). Now you'll need to decide how loose or tight you want your choker to be and how long you would like your bow in the back.

8. Glue or sew vintage buttons or flowers around the choker.

9. To decorate the edge, stack a bead cap, a bead, and then another bead cap on an eyepin and cut the wire ¼ inch above the bead. Make a half-loop with your round-nose pliers at the top of the eye pin. Pull the half-loop through the trim on the choker and then close the loop with the pliers, creating a plain loop. (Refer to page 52 for help with wire techniques.) Repeat

this process until you have embellished the edge of the trim to your liking.

10. Wear your Goth Girl Choker to your next soirée!

ROCKABILLY DOMINO BELT BRACELET

Need a lucky cuff to wear to your next girls' poker night or to sass up a vintage dress ensemble for an evening out? Use your leftover belt segment from the Goth Girl Choker project to make a cuff.

1. Measure your wrist and subtract one inch from the measurement. (This inch will provide the space you need to create a lace-up connection for your cuff.)

2. Cut out a segment from your belt the length of your key measurement.

3. Cut two strips of trim the same length as your belt segment.

4. Sew or glue the trim along the back length of the top and bottom of the belt segment.

5. With your hole punch, punch two or three holes in a row about ¼ inch in from each end of the belt segment.

6. Attach your grommets in each hole. (Purchase the full package that includes the grommet pliers.)

7. Glue your domino to the center of the belt segment. Glue on plastic flowers or sew on vintage buttons to create your desired cuff design.

8. Lace your satin cord back and forth through each set of grommets (like you would lace up your shoes).

9. Let your cuff dry for 2 hours.

10. Wear your cuff with a cute vintage dress, and you'll increase your chances for a straight flush on poker night!

NAKED LADY PARTIES!
BY SUSAN

Revolutionize your wardrobe by hosting a Naked Lady Party (NLP). These clothes swaps with friends are not only super fun—you replace your tired, outgrown, or simply never-quite-right clothes with fresh new pieces—but they're also absolutely free. It's liberating to get a new favorite skirt or jacket without spending a dime!

Start by sorting through your clothes and shoes, setting aside the ones that get no action. It's a lot easier to let go of stuff when you know someone else is going to love it, not to mention that you'll end up with new clothes in the bargain. Pick a weekend afternoon or evening, invite a group of friends over, and clear a space on the living room floor. Serve drinks and snacks if you like, put music on, and swap away!

TIPS

• Send cute personalized online invites or shrink-art invitations (page 173) to your guest list, and if you're comfortable with the party getting bigger, let everyone know they can bring other friends along. Anywhere between eight and twenty-five people is a good range for an NLP, depending on the size of your place. If you have fewer, there won't be as much to swap, and more than twenty-five guests can become kind of chaotic (but still fun).

• Ask friends to bring a little something for the party along with their cast-off clothes. Try a theme NLP—everyone brings a dessert, or brings a mix CD to exchange in a blind swap.

• Sort everything that's up for grabs into loose categories—put shoes, housewares, jewelry, art supplies, and books in different areas. If you like, pull bigger pieces, like coats, out of the general pile and put them aside.

• If you invite people to come over at a certain time, wait at least a half-hour for latecomers before everyone starts digging into the piles. Enjoy cocktails or just chat before the main event—you'll end up with more to choose from!

• Make *very* sure that everyone's own coats, sweaters, or bags—the ones you don't want to donate— are safely stowed in another area far from the pile! Provide a spare bag for each guest to stash away her choices, so the claimed items don't get reabsorbed into the open-season stuff.

• At the end of the party, ask everyone to help clean up by putting the dregs into bags or boxes to donate to a thrift store. If one of the guests has a car, it would be a lovely gesture to deliver the donations so the hostess doesn't have to.

There are three variations on the rules for a Naked Lady Party:

New York Style (NYS): This is the most disciplined party, with one or two guests acting as narrators. A narrator holds up and describes each piece, and anyone interested tries it on or holds it up to herself. If two or more people want the same thing, it is settled by either an agreement between them or a roomwide vote. The highly coveted items usually get evened out by the end of the soiree, with everyone of the same size or taste getting at least one or two gems. This variation *does* take a while, but it is fun seeing everything piece by piece.

PDX Free-For-All (PFFA): This is the Wild West version, with one or several large piles formed and everyone circling the perimeters and sorting through it all. People usually rotate or switch places after spending a while in the same spot, so they can access fresh goods. It's not as cutthroat as it might sound—if someone sees a shirt that's perfect for a friend, it's handed over or thrown across the pile. Anything that isn't a keeper is returned to the top of the pile for the next round.

Portland Rule of Three: This version melds the structure of NYS with the exuberance of PFFA—guests still pick through the giant piles, but take a mandatory break for a few minutes after finding three things they like (or five, or whatever number is chosen at the beginning of the party). After trying things on, getting a snack, or chatting on the sidelines, it's time for round two. This evens the chances of *everyone* finding cool stuff.

SHRINK-O-RAMA

SHRINK 101

Here are some helpful tips for entering the magical world of shrink art! Rules do not apply and the possibilities are endless. Blank sheets of shrink plastic are available at most major craft stores or online. Remember that your finished piece will shrink to a little less than half its size. For example, a 2-inch circle will shrink to about a ⅞-inch circle. (See Fig. 1.)

We've included a page of fabulous clip art for you to use for your projects. You may want to enlarge the designs on a copier before you trace them, depending on the size you want your finished pieces to be.

1. Using permanent markers instead of colored pencils gives you vibrant and crisp colors.

2. You can use acrylic paint and stamping ink to color your shrink plastic, but you will need to coat the surface with decoupage medium or clear nail polish to protect the finished product.

3. Shrink plastic comes in a variety of colors, including black, white, clear, and brown.

4. Use decorative scissors to add detail to the edges of your shrink art. Using a fancy edge can also hide imperfections that would show on a straight-cut edge.

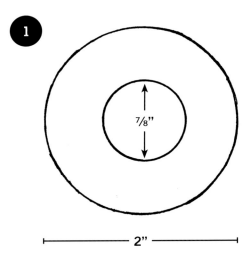

5. Be careful when cutting out your shrink plastic. It can tear easily if you are cutting into tight corners. Try using small manicure scissors.

6. Remember to punch holes *before* shrinking. A standard ¼-inch punch will shrink to the perfect size for jewelry findings.

7. Follow package instructions. Heating times and temperatures vary by brand. Some shrink plastics also have a right and wrong side.

8. If you want to sculpt your shrink plastic into a three-dimensional project, use oven mitts to wrap it around a solid object while the plastic is still hot. (We used a dowel for the ring and a thread spool for the napkin rings.) See Fig. 2.

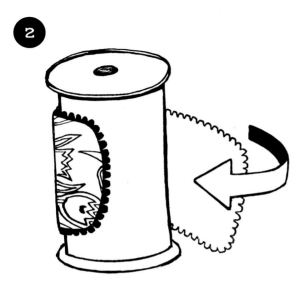

TIPS FOR COMPUTER PRINTING ON SHRINK PLASTIC

1. Carefully read the shrink plastic package instructions.

2. Set your printer for a transparency.

3. Set your printer to print at 50 percent or half tone. The colors may look washed out but will become vibrant when the piece shrinks.

Warning: Never, ever, put shrink plastic through a laser printer or copy machine that uses heat to set the ink. See Crafty Disasters on page 14 for the whole story!

9. A toaster oven is convenient for making shrink art. It heats up faster, and you can slide pieces in and out without burning yourself.

10. Place your shrink art colored side up on a nonstick cookie sheet or pan. This will prevent it from sticking. Or use aluminum foil on a regular cookie sheet or pan.

11. Occasionally your shrink art will curl and stick to itself. You can usually pry it apart with a spatula while it is still hot.

12. Use a spatula to flatten curled edges while the piece is still hot.

13. Remove your shrink art pieces from the oven as soon as they are completely shrunk. They will start to discolor if left in too long.

14. Allow the pieces to cool before trying to remove them from the cookie sheet. They will pop right off when cooled.

15. Use decoupage medium or clear nail polish to protect your finished shrink art from wear and tear.

RETRO BRACELET + CHOKER SET

BY CATHY

YOU'LL NEED

Eight circles cut out of shrink plastic, each 2 inches in diameter

Cool images to trace or draw onto your circles (use the kids' faces on the clip art page, or design your own set)

Ultrafine-tip permanent markers (or colored pencils)

Decoupage medium or clear nail polish

Twelve jump rings

Two clasps (see Jewelry 101 on page 52 to make your own)

13–17 inches of chain for choker (depending on how long you want your necklace to be)

TOOLS

Scissors

1/4-inch hole punch

Cookie sheet

Spatula

Paintbrush (if you're using decoupage medium)

Jewelry pliers

I still remember peering through the window of our toaster oven and watching in awe as my first attempt at shrink art curled up, then flattened to half its original size. I was six years old when my obsession with shrink plastic began. Whoever invented this incredible art form, I salute you! With a blank sheet of shrink plastic and some brightly colored permanent markers (or colored pencils) you can create just about anything—including this cute retro bracelet and choker set. Shrink art is not just for kids anymore, so fire up the toaster oven and shrink away!

1. Place your shrink plastic circles over your image and trace with markers or pencils. Color in any areas that need filling. Repeat until all eight circles are complete. Seven circles will make up the bracelet and one will be for the choker.

2. Use your hole punch to make holes on either side of the image. Since they will shrink, a standard ¼-inch hole works best.

RETRO CHOKER

RETRO BRACELET

3. Shrink away! Follow the manufacturer's instructions included in your shrink plastic package. Allow pieces to completely cool.

4. Coat the colored side of your pieces with decoupage medium or clear nail polish to protect the images from wear.

5. Set aside the circle you plan to use for the choker along with three jump rings, one clasp, and the chain.

6. Arrange the remaining seven circles in the desired order and use the jewelry pliers to link them together using the jump rings, adding a jump ring to each end. (Refer to Jewelry 101 on page 52 if you need help with this.) Attach the clasp to the jump ring on one of the ends. You now have a super cool bracelet!

You can use any shape desired to make this fabulous set. Squares, ovals, rectangles—be creative!

7. For the choker, cut your chain into two pieces, each half of the desired length. Attach one length of chain to each side of the shrink plastic circle using jump rings. Add the remaining jump ring to one end and the clasp to the other and your choker is finished. Enjoy!

SPANISH DANCER EARRINGS

ELEPHANT EARRINGS

SPANISH DANCER + ELEPHANT EARRINGS

BY TORIE/SUSAN

YOU'LL NEED

Shrink plastic

Permanent markers (in the colors of your choice)

Ear wires

Decoupage medium or clear nail polish

2 inches of chain and two jump rings (for dangly earrings)

TOOLS

Scissors

1/4-inch hole punch

Cookie sheet

Spatula

Paintbrush (if you're using decoupage medium)

Jewelry pliers

Torie: I hadn't tried shrink art since childhood, but I must admit, it's a blast! There is something about coloring on plastic, and then watching it writhe and shrink in the oven, that brings out your innermost child.

Susan: I have always wanted a pair of pink elephant earrings, and now I finally have them! I love shrink art.

To make the elephant or dancer earrings pictured, just trace the designs on the page of clip art on 162 in whatever size you want and color them in the combinations desired. Or, if you like to draw, create your own design.

1. Draw, trace, or print (be sure to use the plastic made to run through your printer!) an image onto the shrink plastic and color as desired. You will need two pieces of art if you would like to make a pair of earrings. Cut them out carefully.

2. Punch a hole above or in your design to attach it to the ear wires.

See Jewelry 101 on page 52 for instructions on basic jewelry techniques to attach your shrink art to your earring hooks.

3. Shrink your plastic according to the manufacturer's instructions.

4. Paint a coat of decoupage medium on the colored side of your artwork to help seal it and to avoid scratching the color off. You can also use clear nail polish.

5. If you want to make dangling earrings, cut a 1-inch piece of chain and open a jump ring. Using jewelry pliers, attach the ring to one end of the chain and put the shrink piece on the ring. Close it and attach the other end of the chain to the ear wire. Repeat for the second earring.

PINUP GIRL MERMAID SHOE CLIPS

BY RACHEL

YOU'LL NEED

Vintage or retro pictures

Opaque shrink plastic

Permanent markers

Decoupage medium or clear nail polish

Two-part epoxy with 4-minute drying time

Metal clips

TOOLS

Scissors

Coffee can bottom or other round object to trace

Paper and pencil

Hot pad/oven mitt

Cookie sheet

Spatula

Small paintbrush (if you're using decoupage medium)

Whenever I'm hunting for a new pair of shoes, I find myself redesigning most everything I see into my perfect pair, almost always with the addition of some kind of amazing retro shoe clips. Then during one of my many shrink art frenzies it dawned on me that I could make my own shoe clips. Use images from our clip art page for your shoe clips or design your own gorgeous ones.

1. Choose a pair of shoes screaming out for shoe clips.

2. Browse through vintage/retro pictures and collect images for your shoe clips. You can draw images freehand or collage together various images on your shrink plastic.

3. Trace or draw the image(s) for your first shoe clip on your shrink plastic, cut them out, and color them with permanent marker. If you want to create shoe clips that mirror one another, simply flip over your first shoe clip design and trace it to create your second shoe

clip design. I followed this process to make sure the mermaid girls were facing each other.

4. Use a coffee can bottom or any other object to trace an 8-inch circle for the base of your shoe clip. I suggest that you trace your first circle on a piece of paper, cut it out, and make sure the circle is in proportion to the shoe clip image(s) you will glue on top. The entire sizing should take place before you shrink. Trace two circles onto shrink plastic using this method and cut them out. Color the circles a solid color to provide a uniform base for your shrink art image(s).

5. Following the instructions on your shrink plastic packaging, place all of your circles on a cookie sheet in the oven, shrink them, take them out, and flatten them as needed by carefully pressing down on them with an oven mitt or spatula.

You can order metal clips from Rio Grande—see Resources on page 279 for more information.

6. Place your other shrink art images on a cookie sheet and repeat step 5.

7. Once your shrink art images have cooled, coat them with decoupage medium or clear nail polish on the colored side to protect the colors.

8. When the polish has dried, mix up a quarter-size amount of two-part epoxy. Carefully glue your shrink art images onto the shoe clip shrink circles. With quick-drying epoxy you will only need to hold the images in place for a few minutes before they dry. Mix up another quarter-size amount and glue the metal clips onto the back of each circle.

9. Attach your shoe clips to a pair of shoes and go swing dancing!

THEME PARTY INVITATIONS

FOR ONE INVITATION, YOU'LL NEED

Two 8-inch by 10-inch sheets of *printer-friendly* shrink plastic (It's probably good to have more on hand, though, in case of any mistakes.)

Clear acrylic spray or clear nail polish

Three jump rings or craft wire

TOOLS

Computer and printer

Scissors

Hole punch

Cookie sheet

Spatula

Oven mitt

Jewelry pliers

I love theme parties! (I've even been known to threaten my guests that they must wear costumes to my themed dress-up parties or I won't let them in the door. Scare tactics work!) **Making your own shrink invitations is a fun way to set the mood for your party and let your guests know of your theme in time to comply!**

1. Design an invitation on your computer, using your own drawings, scanned images, or clip art. Make your design slightly smaller than the actual shrink plastic so that all of the edges print, about 7 inches by 9 inches or so. Include the relevant party details: theme, date, time, place, etc.

2. Print out a test invitation on plain paper to make sure it looks good.

3. Print the invitation on your shrink plastic.

4. Cut around the perimeter of the invitation to establish the shape you would like it to be. Leave space at the bottom to punch three holes from which three objects will dangle.

5. Choose three images on your computer of objects that fit with your party theme. For my Naked Lady Party invitation (see page 157), I chose a skirt, a shoe, and a handbag. Place the three items in an 8-inch by 10-inch blank document. To save space, try to fit all three objects on one page. If they don't all fit, you can print them out individually on separate pieces of shrink plastic. Print them out on a sheet of plain paper as a test first.

6. Once you are pleased with the design, print out the three images on a sheet of shrink plastic.

7. Cut out each of the three objects, leaving room above each one to punch a hole.

8. Punch a hole above each object, then punch three corresponding holes on the bottom of your printed invitation where you'd like the objects to dangle from.

9. Preheat the oven according to the instructions on your shrink plastic packaging.

10. Place all of your invitation pieces on a cookie sheet and shrink them, following the shrink-plastic package instructions. Use a spatula to flatten out any stubborn edges. Allow pieces to completely cool before removing them from the pan.

11. In a well-ventilated area, spray one coat of clear acrylic spray on each piece and allow them to dry for about an hour. Repeat if desired. You can also coat the invitation with clear nail polish.

12. Attach each of the three objects to the main invitation using the wire techniques described in Jewelry 101 on page 52.

MY FAVORITE FABRIC NAPKIN RINGS

BY CATHY

YOU'LL NEED

Pretty fabric to scan
(I scanned my favorite
vintage dress.)

One sheet *printer-friendly*
white shrink plastic

Large empty thread spool,
about 1-1/2 inches in
diameter

Decoupage medium or
clear nail polish

TOOLS

Computer and printer

Plain or decorative
scissors

Nonstick cookie sheet

Spatula

Oven mitt

Small paintbrush (if you're
using decoupage medium)

This project brings shrink art to a completely new and amazing level. While the shrink plastic is still hot, you can mold it to any shape you want. In this case, you wrap a long strip around a thread spool to create a napkin ring. I'm really not kidding when I say that the possibilities are endless with shrink art!

1. Scan your fabric into the computer and size it to the same size of your shrink page, less a ¼-inch border on all sides. If you don't have a scanner, you can go to a copy shop to have it scanned and put on a disc. Do not put shrink plastic through a copy machine! (See Crafty Disasters on page 14 for details.)

2. Print your image out onto the shrink page. Be sure to follow the printing instructions given with your printer-friendly shrink plastic and refer to Shrink 101 on page 160.

3. Trim off the unprinted edges and cut the remaining printed piece into four equal-size vertical strips with rounded corners. Each

piece should be about 2 inches wide and 10 inches long. Use decorative scissors to give your napkin rings a fancy edge. I used scalloped-edge scissors on mine.

4. Preheat your oven to the temperature given on your shrink plastic package. You will shrink your napkin rings one at a time in order to carefully wrap them into shape. Place one strip, color side down, onto a nonstick cookie sheet, and put it in the preheated oven. You want to place the strip color side down so that you can easily wrap it around the spool and have the color on the outside of the napkin ring.

5. When the strip has completely shrunk and flattened, you will need to act fast. Pull the oven tray out a little and carefully but quickly wrap the soft strip around the thread spool. It will be extremely hot but once it starts to cool,

I used my computer to create a template that made the black edges on my napkin rings. If you want to try this, simply create an oblong shape with a thick line (remember, it will be much thinner once it shrinks) and combine it with your scanned image in a program like Photoshop or Freehand. After you print it out, cut along the black line with decorative scissors. It gives the napkin rings a nice, defined edge.

it will no longer be pliable. Use a spatula and oven mitt to hold the strip in place around the spool while you remove it from the oven and let it cool. The shrink should harden within a few seconds.

6. Repeat steps 4 and 5 with the remaining three pieces.

7. Coat the napkin rings with clear nail polish so the ink will not run. (You can also brush on decoupage medium.)

VAMP GIRL POWER RING

BY RACHEL

YOU'LL NEED

Shrink plastic (for this project I used opaque instead of clear)

A variety of permanent fine-tip markers

Vintage or new images from magazines, books, or old advertisements

Decoupage medium or clear nail polish

TOOLS

Scissors

Cookie sheet

Spatula

Hot pads, oven mitts, or thick cotton gloves

A wooden dowel the size of your ring finger (Ask a hardware store employee to cut a 3-inch section of your dowel. You can also carefully do this at home with a handsaw.)

Small paintbrush (if you're using decoupage medium)

In a magical sense, wearing a ring "binds" you with power and with energy. The imagery and materials you use to create a ring can determine the nature of this energy. Historically, many rings were worn on the third finger because it was thought to contain a nerve that went directly to the heart. With that said, I say forget the Power Suit and the Power Lunch—every girl needs a Power Ring. For design inspiration, see our ideas on the clip art page 162.

1. I strongly suggest some experimentation with the shrink art plastic and bending process before bending your final ring. The techniques in steps 2–7 will determine your ring size.

2. Cut three strips from your shrink art plastic: 4, 5, and 6 inches long. Write the length with permanent marker on each of your strips.

3. Following the instructions on your shrink plastic package, place one strip at a time on a cookie sheet in the preheated oven.

4. Once the strip has shrunk, continue to let it heat up. Your goal is to continue to heat it so that it is pliable.

5. Protect your hands with oven mitts, hot pads, or thick cotton gloves as you remove the first strip of shrink art from the oven and wrap the strip around your wooden dowel. If the strip stiffens up, place it back in the oven to heat up. If it is wrapped around the dowel, but not completely rounded, place the dowel with the strip in the oven. When you see the strip moving as it heats up, again quickly take the dowel out of the oven and press the strip around it.

6. Repeat step 5 with other strips as needed until you determine the right length to create your ring.

7. Cut out the strip you will use for your final Power Ring.

8. Gather your images or sketch out your Power Ring design on pieces of scrap paper.

You may want to adorn your toe instead of your finger. All you need to do is ask your local hardware clerk to cut a dowel the size of one of your lovely toes!

Remember, you can combine imagery using collage techniques. I used an image of flowers from an old advertisement with images of spiders from a book on insects to create some of the designs on my power ring.

9. Once you have completed your design with permanent markers, place your strip onto a cookie sheet in the preheated oven. Repeat step 5 until you have successfully formed your strip into a ring. You may need to spend 10–20 minutes heating and reheating your strip and forming the strip around the dowel.

10. Paint your ring with a coat of clear nail polish or decoupage medium.

11. Wear your Power Ring and you will most certainly rock!

CRAFTY PETS

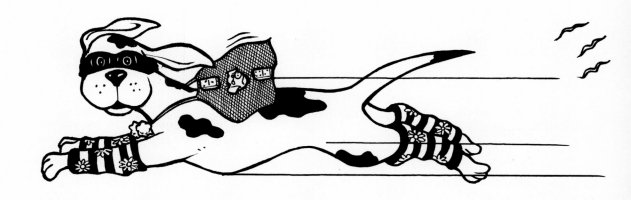

ROCK + ROLL KITTY TOY

YOU'LL NEED

Two 3-1/2-inch black felt circles

White thread

Two 1-1/2-inch brightly colored felt circles

Black thread

3 tablespoons dried catnip

TOOLS

Sewing machine or needle and thread, if you're hand-sewing

1/4-inch hole punch

Straight pins

Scissors

If you're like me, you're tired of the same old catnip toys for your cat. The fish and the mouse have been way overdone. Cats want something cooler. Wow your felines with this hip toy that will turn them into rock stars!

1. Use your white thread to stitch a spiral from the outer edge inward on each of the two black felt circles to resemble the grooves in a record.

2. Use the hole punch to make a hole in the center of each of the smaller brightly colored felt circles to resemble the hole in the center of the record.

3. Pin the colored felt circles to the right side of each of the black felt circles, making sure they are centered. Use your black thread to stitch around the outer edge of the colored circles, attaching them to the black circles.

4. Next, pin the two finished records wrong sides together and stitch around the outer edge, leaving a two-inch opening for the catnip.

5. Stuff the catnip through the opening, then finish stitching it up.

6. Now sit back and watch your cats go crazy!

For extra cuteness, cut musical notes out of brightly colored felt and hand-stitch them onto the finished product.

If, after a few weeks, your kitty has grown bored with the toy, you can open the seam with a seam ripper, replace the catnip with some potent new stuff, and stitch it back up.

PRETTY KITTY COLLAR

BY CATHY

YOU'LL NEED

One strip pink vinyl, 1 inch by 11 inches

One strip black vinyl with felt backing, 1 inch by 11 inches

One 3-inch piece of 3/4-inch-wide black elastic

One vest buckle (available at fabric stores)

TOOLS

Scissors and pinking shears

Ruler

Star-shaped hole punch

Sewing machine with contrasting thread

There's nothing cuter than a well-accessorized cat. Make this collar for your favorite pretty kitty and he or she will be the coolest cat on your block.

For tips on sewing with vinyl, see Vinyl 101 (page 226).

1. Use the scissors to cut a point at one end of both strips of vinyl.

2. Starting 1 inch from the flat end, punch star shapes 1 inch apart along the center of the pink vinyl strip. Punch a cluster of three stars at the pointed end. Keep in mind that your stitching will be 3/16 inch from the edge, so don't punch your stars too close to where the seam will be.

3. Loop the elastic around the center bar of the vest buckle and stitch it together, leaving a long tail of elastic to attach to the collar.

4. Place the pink vinyl strip on top of the black vinyl so that the black shows through the stars and the soft felt back is on the inside of the collar. Place the elastic end between the two vinyl layers at the flat end of the collar and stitch it into place. Continue sewing all around the edge of the vinyl using a $\frac{3}{16}$-inch seam allowance. Double check your measurements to make sure that the collar will fit exactly into the buckle when it is trimmed.

5. Now you are going to trim the edges, one layer at a time. With plain scissors, trim the pink vinyl all around the edge of the collar to within $\frac{1}{8}$ inch of the seam. You can do this easily by folding the black layer under and holding it while you trim the upper layer. Next,

It is important to make your collar so that it will give or release if your kitty is stuck on a branch or something. That is why I used both the elastic and the vest buckle, which easily slides loose when you pull on it.

use pinking shears to trim the black vinyl layer, leaving the zig-zag edge showing below the straight pink edge. Trim the pointed end of the collar with regular scissors, still leaving the black vinyl a little longer so that it sticks out from under the pink.

ROSIE'S FOUR-LEGGED WARMERS

BY RACHEL

YOU'LL NEED

Dog

Dog treats

1 yard of 1/4-inch-wide elastic

Old cotton/Lycra shirt

Vintage appliqués of your choice (I used flowers from an old dress)

TOOLS

Fabric measuring tape

Pen and paper

Scissors

Fabric marker or chalk

Needle and thread

Sewing machine (optional)

Small safety pin

Dogs need legwarmers too! Rosie is a shorthaired English bulldog who gets rather chilly in the cold winter months here in Portland. She has a collection of sweaters, but until this breakthrough in dog attire, her poor legs would start shaking on our afternoon strolls. I want to assure you this is not a case of a human trying to impose people clothes onto a dog—you know, when people dress their poor dogs in baseball hats or little suits with bow ties. Four-legged warmers are utilitarian accessories that keep your dog cozy and instantly make him or her the talk of the neighborhood.

1. Measure the circumference and length of each of your dog's four legs and write down these measurements. Make sure to have plenty of treats on hand to complete this step.

2. Pull the elastic around the top and bottom of each leg to test the size. The elastic should fit snugly, but in no way should it cut off the

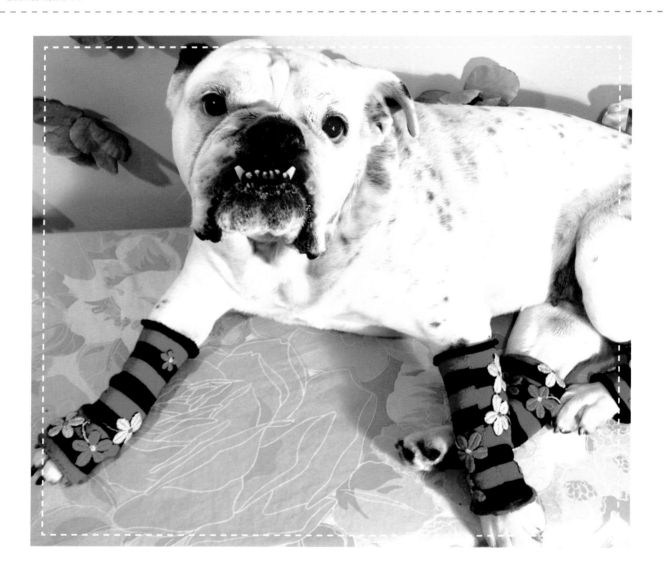

circulation of your doggy's legs. The elastic will help to hold the legwarmers in place.

3. With scissors, cut apart the seams of an old cotton/Lycra shirt (you can also use stretchy tights). Draw out measurements for one legwarmer on your old shirt or tights. Cut four pieces out of your fabric based upon the measurements of your dog's legs. Make sure to add ½-inch to each width measurement to allow enough room for sewing the pieces into tubes. Add 1 inch to the length of each tube to leave enough room for the elastic that will be inserted at the top and bottom of each legwarmer.

4. Hand-sew vintage appliqués as desired onto each of the four pieces of fabric.

5. Hand- or machine-sew your first piece together into a tube inside out so the stitching is on the inside. Fold the top over ½ inch and sew the circumference of the tube, stopping when you have a ½-inch space left open. Attach a small safety pin to one side of one piece of elastic and run it through the top of the legwarmer, while holding the other end of the elastic. Hand-sew both ends of the elastic together and then sew up the open space on the legwarmer. Repeat this step until you have completed all four legwarmers. Turn each one right side out.

6. With doggie treats in hand, pull each legwarmer onto your dog's legs and go for a stroll on a cold winter day.

MEOW DOG HAT

YOU'LL NEED

Vintage velvet hat

Dog

Dog treats

Vintage rose trim

Vintage stuffed cat (or other animal) head

TOOLS

Fabric measuring tape

Scissors

Needle and thread

My bulldog Greta has an affinity for cats, and for what comes out of cats, if you know what I mean. She loves what one neighbor has aptly called her cat treat, Kitty Roca. One year for Halloween I decided to symbolize Greta's immense fascination with cats by creating the Meow Dog Hat for her.

1. Find a soft fabric vintage hat.

2. Place the hat snugly on your dog's head and measure from the bottom of each side of the hat to under your dog's head. Give your dog a treat or two. Add 7 inches to this measurement to determine how long to make the two strips of trim that will tie under your dog's head to hold the hat in place. Cut two strips of trim in this length.

3. Sew one strip of trim onto each side of the hat.

4. Find a vintage stuffed animal that symbolizes something about your dog's personality.

5. Cut the head, or a body part of your choice, off the stuffed animal.

6. Sew the body part onto the front of the hat, or onto any area of your choice.

7. Embellish the hat with vintage trim to your liking.

8. Give your dog a treat and tie the hat onto his or her head.

9. Trick or treat—and try to ease off the Kitty Roca, Greta!

LUCKY PIG DOG CAPE

BY RACHEL

YOU'LL NEED

Small to medium-size dog, any breed

Vintage placemat

2 yards of 1/2-inch or wider satin cord

2 small fabric or rubber balls

1/2 yard of faux fur

Nontoxic glue

Dog treats

A good friend to administer dog treats

1 yard of 1-inch-wide elastic

Velcro

Rubber toy

Vintage black Lucite beads

Dominos or other game pieces

Black ribbon

TOOLS

Scissors

Needle and thread

Measuring tape

Hey all you dog owners out there—you too can craft with your dog! I've always been slightly creeped out when I see pet owners dressing their dogs in suits, sweaters, and just about anything else that resembles human clothing. I would like to invite all of the disenfranchised dog owners of the world to partake in this project and liberate your secret desire to dress your dogs! The ultimate goal is to create a dog cape reflecting your dog's unique personality without embarrassing yourself—and your pooch—by putting him or her in a coat and tie.

Warning: **Your dog must be supervised at all times while wearing a cape.**

1. Go straight to your local thrift store and check out the vintage placemats. They make the perfect base for a fabulous dog cape! Make sure to choose a flexible cloth or yarn placemat so that your cape will drape over your dog to fit comfortably.

2. Cut the satin cord in half (you will need 1–2 yards total, depending on the size of your dog). Hand-sew each piece of cord to each top corner of the placemat.

3. Create puffs by covering the fabric or rubber balls with your faux fur. You can either sew the faux fur onto the balls or use nontoxic glue to attach it. Layer the faux fur over the balls to reach your desired size of puff. Sew each faux-fur puff onto one end of the satin cord.

4. Once again drape the placemat over your dog's back. With the help of dog treats and your friend, measure from one end of the placemat to the other by running the measuring tape under your pet's stomach. You are measuring the length of elastic you will need so that the cape is secured comfortably around your dog's stomach.

5. Cut the elastic to size, leaving 1 extra inch on each side. Sew one end of the elastic to the edge of the placemat. Sew a 1-inch piece of Velcro to the other end of the elastic and sew the matching piece of 1-inch Velcro to the other side of the cape.

6. Embellish your cape by cutting off the head of the rubber toy and gluing the head onto the cape. You can also glue or sew on beads, game pieces, and ribbons to finish off your cape for your dog.

7. Dress up your dog in the new cape and take a stroll around town. Make sure to supervise closely so that your dog does not eat his or her cape.

LE TIGRE DOG CAPE

BY RACHEL

YOU'LL NEED

Stuffed animal

Felt

Vintage necktie

Vintage placemat

TOOLS

Sharp scissors

Needle and thread

1. Filet a stuffed animal of your choice. Cut around the seam of the stuffed animal and remove the stuffing and the bottom half of the animal. I left the stuffing in the head and tail to give the cape a slightly three-dimensional look.

2. Hand-sew the fileted stuffed animal onto an old placemat.

3. Embellish with felt shapes.

4. Cut a vintage necktie into two long strips. Hand-sew the strips to each side of the cape.

5. Tie the cape onto your dog and go for a little walk with your new superhero friend.

GOOD KITTY PET PLACEMAT

Tell your kitty just what you think of him or her with a Good Kitty Pet Placemat. (And keep cat food off your floor as a bonus!)

YOU'LL NEED

20-inch by 14-inch piece of poster paper (or whatever size you would like your placemat to be)

Black, pink, and green felt

Glue

Yellow thread

Alphabet stickers

TOOLS

Pencil

Scissors

Laminating options: clear contact paper, clear vinyl (to sew on), or a laminating machine (a local copy shop can also laminate it for you)

1. Draw scalloped edges onto the back of your poster paper. Cut along the drawn lines so that your paper is now scalloped all the way around.

2. Cut the shape of the kitty head (see Fig. 1) out of black felt.

3. Cut two pink felt triangles for the insides of the ears. The ones shown here are 1 inch by 1 inch by ¾ inch. Make sure you cut them smaller than the actual ear, so you have some black felt showing all the way around the pink triangle. (If you fold your felt in half so you are cutting through two layers at a time, you will cut two triangles of the same size and shape). Glue them onto the kitty ears.

4. Cut two almond shapes out of green felt for the eyes. The ones shown here are 1¼ inches long by ½ inch high at the center. Glue them

onto the black kitty head. Then cut two small slivers out of black felt for the pupils and glue them onto the green eyes.

5. Cut a small triangle out of pink felt, then round the corners to make a nose. Glue the nose onto the kitty head.

6. Cut twelve 5-inch strands of yellow thread for the whiskers. Set them aside.

7. Determine where you would like the kitty's head to be on the placemat and glue it in place.

8. Now it's time to apply the alphabet letters. It's easiest and most accurate to start with the letter(s) in the center of the word and work out from there. Space your letters out evenly.

9. To attach the whiskers, glue the pieces of thread onto the cat's face and placemat where you would like them to be.

10. Laminating options: It's helpful to be able to wipe off a placemat, so you will probably want to cover your placemat either with vinyl, contact paper, or laminating. I had this placemat laminated at the local copy shop,

and then I trimmed the edges to match the scalloping. You could also place contact paper on both the front and back (being careful to roll it out slowly and smoothly across the paper). The other option is to take two pieces of clear vinyl that are larger than your placemat and sew them together with the placemat in the middle.

This makes a wonderful personalized gift. Create your own good doggie placemat, too. You could even add photos of your pet to make a fun collage.

CRAFT MY RIDE

IT'S SPRING! BIKE HELMET

BY SUSAN

YOU'LL NEED

Silk flowers (I used two large stems of fake hydrangeas to cover the entire helmet.)

Silicone sealer glue

Bike helmet

TOOLS

Sharp scissors

Let's face it—bike helmets really don't look very cool. I was so tired of wearing my plain one, which made me feel nerdy, and longed for something cuter . . . when I got the idea to decorate my helmet in the style of a vintage swim cap covered with blossoms. This project takes a grand total of 15 minutes (not counting the time it takes the glue to dry), and after you've fancied up your helmet, it'll feel like spring year-round.

1. Cut off the flowers you're using about ¼ inch below the blossom, so a very short piece of stem remains on each one. Don't cut too close or the flower may fall apart. Sort the flowers into smaller and larger if their sizes vary. We'll glue the larger ones on first.

2. Apply a large glob of silicone sealer on the front of the helmet. Place a larger flower on the glob and press so the stem is anchored in the glue. Add another glob about an inch away and glue on a second flower. Cover the helmet with flowers using this technique, mixing in other colors or kinds if you like. If any fall off, just reattach them with more glue.

3. After you've done one layer of flowers, add smaller ones to cover any spaces. Let the helmet dry overnight.

4. Ride around town looking stylish.

If you're a fan of florals, why not make some Felt Flowers (page 67), Rosie's Four-Legged Warmers (page 187), a Sultry Slip (page 141), or even Flirty Floral Pasties (page 61)?

This helmet is perfect for skating paired with Daisy Skates (page 213).

LADYBUG BIKE HELMET

BY SUSAN

YOU'LL NEED

1/4 yard stretchy black fabric

1/4–1/3 yard stretchy red fabric

Bike helmet

Drawstring and stopper

Six 2-inch black felt circles

12-inch piece of 1/2-inch-wide black ribbon

Strong glue

Googly eyes

TOOLS

Straight pins

Sewing machine

Sharp scissors

Large safety pin or elastic guide

Needle and thread

As I mentioned before, bike helmets sadly lag far behind the rest of our wardrobes in terms of attractiveness. If you want a style infusion with the option of going back to plain-jane in no time, this removable ladybug slipcover is just the thing. This pattern is not universal, since helmets vary a lot in size and shape, but you can adapt it to cover yours—the stretchy fabric covers a multitude of sins!

Refer to Sewing 101 on page 22 if you need a few pointers. I also recommend using a stretch needle and stretch or zig-zag stitch setting on your sewing machine.

1. Pin the pieces of red and black fabric together and machine-sew them along the edge to form a large rectangle that is approximately one-third black and two-thirds red (see Fig. 1A). Drape this piece over your helmet (as shown in Fig. 1B). My helmet was 16 inches wide by 22 inches long, so my rectangle was originally 22 inches wide by 30 inches long, for example. Use sharp scissors to cut the fabric from a rectangle into a rough

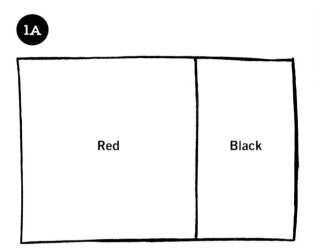

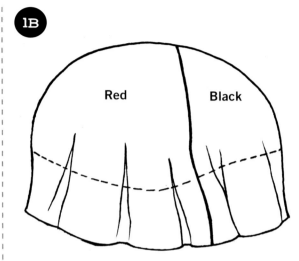

oval that is larger than the helmet but follows its shape, as shown Fig. 1B. The black section will cover the front of the helmet and the red section will cover the back.

2. Take the fabric off the helmet and begin folding the edge over about an inch, wrong sides together, to form a channel which will eventually hold the drawstring. Pin this fold and continue folding and pinning all the way around the oval, gathering fabric together when there is excess. Place the fabric back

over the helmet and, keeping in mind that it will stretch, eye it to make sure it will cover the helmet. Adjust the fold if it is too big or too small in places.

3. Starting at the narrow end of the red side of the oval, begin machine-sewing on the pinned fabric, leaving a $5/8$-inch channel. Continue around the entire oval and backstitch at the beginning and end of the seam to hold it, leaving a 1- to 2-inch opening.

4. Using your elastic guide or safety pin, slowly guide the drawstring through the channel. When it is drawn through the entire passage, slip the stopper over both ends of the string. Put the slipcover on the helmet and pull the drawstring taut to secure it.

5. Pin the six felt circles onto the back of the ladybug in a symmetrical pattern (as shown in the photograph) to form its spots. Hand-sew them on with needle and thread. Lay the

Believe it or not, you can make matching Ladybug Lovin' Pasties (page 64) for a truly show-stopping ensemble!

ribbon down the middle of the back to divide the red section in half and attach it with strong glue.

6. Attach the googly eyes on the black section with strong glue. Let the eyes and ribbon set overnight.

COWGIRL DRIVIN' MACHINE

BY RACHEL

YOU'LL NEED

Black fabric steering wheel cover

3 yards black fringe trim

3 yards light pink (or the color of your choice) fringe trim

3 yards vintage or new flower-pattern trim

Vintage or new appliqué

Newspaper or butcher paper

Fabric glue

Masking tape

Any kind of car

TOOLS

Scissors

Back in my early teenage years, there seemed to be a weird phenomenon involving low-rider Volkswagens with chain steering wheels. I remember feeling strangely drawn to this unique group of cars that regularly cruised Main Street on Friday nights in my town. For anyone else who harbors a secret desire to alter their auto, this is a simple project offering you the opportunity to live out some teenage dreams.

1. Go to your local auto supply store and purchase a new plain black steering wheel cover. Visit your local craft store or thrift shop to pick out your fringe and flower patterned trims. You will need three yards of each type of trim to ensure you have plenty to encircle your steering wheel cover. (You can also bring the steering wheel cover with you to measure exactly how much trim you will need.) Buy a vintage or new appliqué that complements the color scheme of your trim.

2. Cover a table with newspaper or butcher paper.

3. Wrap the black trim around the outside of the steering wheel cover and cut to size.

4. Squeeze a thick layer of fabric glue on the back of the black fringe. Smooth the fabric glue with your finger so that the layer of glue is consistent on the back of the fringe.

5. Glue the fringe around the outside of the steering wheel cover. Tape the fringe in place on the steering wheel cover with masking tape. Let the fringe dry for 1 hour.

6. Take your next strip of fringe, in pink or the color of your choice, and cover the back top edge with fabric glue. Glue the trim onto the top strip of the black fringe to create a layered multicolored steering wheel edge. Tape in place with masking tape and let dry for 1 hour.

Other options for dressing up your steering wheel include covering a standard steering wheel cover with vintage fabric, a recycled knit sweater (just cut off the long sleeves and sew them into a knit tube over the steering wheel cover), and covering the steering wheel with Felt Flowers (see page 67). Just make sure you don't get too carried away and create a steering wheel that is a driving hazard. You can look downright cool and still be safe.

7. Repeat step 6 with your third piece of trim.

8. Cover the back of your appliqué with fabric glue. Carefully press the appliqué onto the top of the steering wheel to finish your steering wheel design. Let dry for 1 hour.

9. Put your steering wheel cover on and go for a cruise down Main Street!

DAISY SKATES

BY RACHEL

YOU'LL NEED

Roller skates

Silk flowers

Opaque knee-high nylons

Velcro

TOOLS

Hot glue gun with 15 refill glue sticks

Scissors

Needle and thread

When I was in middle school I had these incredible blue puffs with bells in the middle that attached to my roller skate laces. I also had a pair of gold lamé wings that attached around each of my ankles and a red satin spectator jacket with a black panther on the back. Now that I am a little older and much more low-key, I sport my Daisy Skates for jaunts around town. Go ahead and get crafty with your skates!

1. Immediately go out and buy roller skates if you don't already own a pair. Pick out flowers from your local thrift or craft store. Buy a pair of knee-high nylons or socks to match the color of the shoe or boot of your skates.

2. Plug in your glue gun and make sure you have at least 15 glue sticks to refill it.

3. Cut off the stem of each flower.

4. Slip the knee-high over each skate.

5. Carefully make small incisions with your

scissors to create holes for your skate brakes and wheels.

6. Sew small pieces of Velcro near the top of your nylons and near the foot opening of your skates. They will help hold the nylons in place if you experience slippage.

7. Once your skates are completely covered by the nylons, begin attaching the flowers.

8. Squeeze out hot glue onto the back of a flower, pull the nylon away from the skate shoe, and carefully press the flower into the

Are your Daisy Skates crying out for more skating accessories? How about making some Pretty Paper + Fabric hair clips on page 81, some adorable POW! Wristbands on page 151, or an It's Spring! Bike Helmet on page 203? Now you are ready to roller boogie!

nylon until the glue cools. Repeat this step until both skates are covered with flowers.

9. Put on your skates and a sassy outfit and live it up!

SHOW-STOPPING CAR CURTAIN

YOU'LL NEED

Felt piece to fit the length of your windshield (mine was 46 inches by 7-1/2 inches)

1-1/2 to 2 yards fringe or tassel trim

2 yards Velcro (with one half adhesive and the other half sew-on)

Two images that you love, 1-1/2 inches wide by 2 inches tall

Two pieces clear vinyl, 1-3/4 inches wide by 2-1/4 inches tall

Two pieces solid-colored vinyl, 2 inches wide by 2-1/2 inches tall (cut with pinking shears if you like)

Double-stick tape

Assorted trinkets—I used plastic horseshoes and musical notes, velvet leaves and flowers, and a good-luck penny

TOOLS

Measuring tape

Paper and pencil

Scissors

Sewing machine

Hot glue gun

The first thing I did when I got my hand-me-down used truck was figure out how I was going to put fringe in the windshield—I felt like the car wasn't really mine until I added my own special touch to it. You can use these directions to fancify your car with a traffic-stopping windshield decoration that reflects your personal style. Here are specific instructions for the one I made for my car, but feel free to stray from them to create your own one-of-a-kind moving masterpiece.

1. First, measure your windshield to see how wide you need to make your curtain. It is important that you measure accurately. Figure out where you will attach the Velcro and add about a 1-inch allowance around the edge. I attached my Velcro to the small ceiling ledge just above my windshield. You also need to sit in your car and figure out exactly how low the curtain can hang without impairing your vision. (Mine hangs down about 6 inches.)

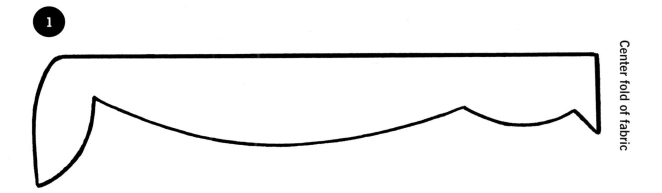

Center fold of fabric

2. Using the general shape from Fig. 1 and the measurements that you took from your car, make a pattern out of paper. The curtain has to be exactly the right size to fit correctly in the window, so double- and triple-check your measurements and hold the paper pattern in the window before you cut out the felt.
As you can see in the diagram, you will have one center piece that hangs down behind the rearview mirror and two sides that will taper down. The pieces between the edges and the center can be any style or shape you want.
I used one large curve that hangs down, but you could also do a series of curves that give a scalloped look. I can't stress enough the importance of not letting the curtain hang down too low. You definitely don't want to impair your visibility or compromise your safety for the sake of being fancy!

3. Once you have finalized your paper pattern, place it on a folded piece of felt with the "center fold" edge on the fold and use it to cut out your felt piece. Remember that the pattern is only half of the final piece.

4. Sew the fringe trim all along the lower edge of the felt curtain. The side that you sew the fringe onto will be the decorated side that will face into your car. (If you're feeling inspired, decorate both sides!)

5. Next, you will need to stitch the sew-on

half of the Velcro onto the felt. I sewed a solid strip all along the top of the curtain and used smaller 2-inch pieces to attach the corners and sides, but you will need to decide what will work best for the corner curves of your particular car. You will need to cut both parts of Velcro in the same sizes, but set aside the adhesive part until the next step.

6. Stick the adhesive part of the Velcro to the inside of your car. The best way to do this is to stick the two Velcro parts together, then bring the entire curtain out to your car. Hold the curtain up and determine how you are going to position it. The Velcro will adhere to the ledge above your windshield while the decorated side of the curtain hangs facing into the car. Peel off the adhesive backing and slowly stick the Velcro to the inside of the car, starting from the center and moving out to each side. The reason you should do this step before you attach any of the trinkets is because you need to see the curtain in the car to know what will look good. You can note where the mirror is to get an idea for placement.

You can buy wide felt by the yard at most fabric stores. You might even luck out like I did and find felt with glitter in it! If you are feeling really adventurous, you can create several curtains and change them with the seasons. Don't you just love Velcro?

Measuring your windshield can be tough—just be sure to take the corner curves into consideration.

I know I said it before, but make sure your curtain doesn't impair your driving in any way! You don't ever want to have to say the words, "I'm sorry, officer, I couldn't see because the fringe was in the way."

7. Remove the curtain, leaving the adhesive part of the Velcro in place. Now that all the calculating and measuring is done, you can begin the creative process of decorating your curtain.

8. Next, assemble the pictures. Center one image on a piece of solid-colored vinyl, using the tape to keep it in place. Put the clear vinyl piece on top of the image, making sure it is centered. Stitch the clear vinyl in place, carefully sewing around the edge of the image. Make two of these vinyl-covered pictures, one for each side.

9. Lay your curtain out and experiment with placement of your trinkets and vinyl pictures. Once you have decided on your design, attach them with a glue gun. I'm a symmetrical kind of girl, so I glued things on my curtain in a mirror image. I hung one special thing in the center, just below my rearview mirror—a good-luck penny from 1956. You can make it as simple or wild as you want it to be.

10. You are finally done! Hang your curtain in your car and proudly cruise around town. You are guaranteed to turn some heads!

GOOD JUJU MIRROR CHARM

YOU'LL NEED

Two playing cards (or any lucky images the size of playing cards, 2-1/4 inches by 3-1/2 inches)

Clear or tinted vinyl, 10-1/2 inches by 6-1/2 inches

Double-stick tape

13 inches decorative trim for first (inner) row

14 inches decorative trim for second (outer) row

11 inches thin elastic cord

TOOLS

Sewing machine or needle and thread

Scissors, decorative or plain

Grommet pliers with one 1/4-inch brightly colored grommet (Optional—you can also just use a hole punch.)

Everyone needs a little good juju in their car. Whether it's finding a good parking space or avoiding a speeding ticket, luck is a wonderful thing. Make this mobile good-luck piece out of vinyl, some scraps of trim that look good from both sides, and a favorite lucky image, and then hang it in your car and watch the good luck pour on in. Every little bit helps!

1. Stick your two images or cards together back-to-back using the tape.

2. Now fold the piece of clear vinyl in half widthwise. Center the image between the layers of vinyl. You should have a 1½-inch border of vinyl left on all sides.

3. Carefully sew (either by hand or by machine) all around the image, getting as close as you can to the edge. Refer to Vinyl 101 on page 226 for helpful tips.

4. Cut open the folded vinyl edge.

5. Starting at the top center, place the end of your first row of trim between the two layers of vinyl. You want the trim to be as close to the sewn seam as possible. Hold the trim in place while you sew another seam on the outside edge of it. You may have to insert a few inches at a time, sew, and then repeat in order to get the trim as close to the first sewn edge as possible. Curve the trim around the corners to make a rounded edge. When you end up back at the top, neatly overlap the ends and finish sewing the seam around it.

6. Repeat step 5 with the second row of trim. You will want to leave a small space (about ¼ inch) between the ends at the top center for the hole.

7. If you don't have grommet pliers, use your hole punch to make a hole in the center top. If you do have grommet pliers, use it to punch a small hole in the center top. Insert the grommet into the hole and use the pliers to fasten it.

8. Trim the excess vinyl from the edges using plain scissors or pinking shears.

9. Tie the two ends of the thin elastic cord in a knot. Now you have a knotted end and a folded end. Insert the folded end through the grommet hole and then place the knotted end through this loop. Pull the cord tightly.

10. Hang it in your car and enjoy that good juju!

The measurements I give for the clear vinyl piece are slightly bigger than you'll need, but I found that having a little extra room helped prevent mistakes. Don't worry about lining the edges up perfectly because you just can trim them neatly when you are done.

CRAFTS ON THE GO!

BY SUSAN

I love traveling almost as much as I love crafting, but I've learned the hard way that the two don't always mix! I've dropped seed beads all over the car floor, had a marker malfunction leak ink everywhere on a long flight, and lost my half-finished project somewhere along the way. But if you bring along the right craft, your trip can be so much more fun.

After college, I traveled all over Europe by train making jewelry, and met so many cool people who saw what I was working on and wanted to chat. I also sold quite a few pieces, or traded them for food, drinks, or books in English, another major bonus. When I drove cross-country to move to Oregon, I hand-sewed and altered a few T-shirts while it was my friend's turn to drive—it was a labor of love, but really fun, and the hours just flew by while I was working on them.

TIPS

• Keep your supplies limited and organized. Don't bring *all* your beads with you, or every single strand of embroidery thread you own: Choose what you want to work with and leave the rest at home.

• A plastic organizer with little compartments and a tight lid is perfect for jewelry supplies or embroidery gear.

• If you're flying, use a nail clipper instead of scissors to snip yarn or thread. Cut out anything you can before you leave, too.

• A small tray or lid can be a great work surface in a car.

Here are the best crafts for taking across town or around the world—thanks to the wonderful craftistas of **www.getcrafty.com** for adding their suggestions!

BEST PORTABLE CRAFTS

Jewelrymaking and beading
Knitting (especially on circular needles)
Crochet
Macrame
Origami
Drawing or writing in a sketchbook or journal
Hand-sewing (I made twenty Felt Flowers [see page 67] during a road trip to California last year)
  Cross-stitching, embroidery, or needlepoint

LEAVE AT HOME

Anything involving things that spill or stain—glue, paint, ink, or water
Anything toxic—glues, glazes, or chemicals
Anything heavy or especially fragile
Anything you would be devastated to lose

Happy trails!

ARTCARS

BY SUSAN

I asked my friend Joanne Owens, crafter and ArtCars artiste, a few questions about her incredible art truck, Bruce.

What is Bruce adorned with, and how did you fancify him?
He's primarily covered with scraps of fabric in jewel tones. I glued them on the body of the truck with spray adhesive, all with straight lines around the various random shapes. I glued black ribbon along all the "seams" of the fabric, doing a kind of stained-glass quilt effect, and added purple faux fur to the hood and tailgate.

I did the fabric outside first, and some feathery trim around the base of the camper shell. I also decorated the inside of the camper shell, turning it into my little retreat. I put in a rug and pinned a purple gauzy fabric on the roof of the shell, letting it hang down on the sides and tenting it. I added some brocade and chenille pillows. All of that can come out if need be. Even the fabric tenting is just rough Velcro safety-pinned to the fabric, which sticks to the inside roof of the camper shell.

I also bought purple seat covers online, with matching dashboard and steering wheel covers. Recently, I got about 7,000 purple rhinestones that I am using to slowly cover the front and rear bumpers—I'm attaching them with silicone glue.

Any tips?
You really can't go wrong with an ArtCar, barring damaging something mechanical on the car, or creating a place where water can leak in.

There are certain things you need to ensure to keep it street legal: working lights, visibility for the driver, some size guidelines, clearances . . . but apart from that, once you check your state codes, anything goes!

I definitely recommend getting involved with ArtCar events. You meet a lot of fun, artistic, interesting people, and the impact of an ArtCar caravan on the roads is great! Also, it gives you opportunities for traveling to different festivals, which can include visiting schools and children's hospitals to show your cars—it's really rewarding.

Which websites or organizations are helpful for finding ArtCar events and resources?
• **www.ArtCarFest.com** is the Bay Area festival.

• **www.ArtCars.com** is Harrod Blank's website. He's one of the patron saints of ArtCars—he's made two films and written a couple of books on them.

• There is a great Yahoo group, artcarz, as well.

VINYL
ADVENTURES

VINYL 101

Tips on sewing with vinyl:

1. Machine-sewing is the only way to go. When you sew on vinyl surfaces, there is a drag created by the friction between your sewing machine presser foot and the sticky fabric. To avoid this, you need to put an additional layer between the foot and the vinyl. There are several ways to create this additional layer:

A. I used a clear plastic grocery bag on my Viva Oilcloth Placemats (page 87). I could still see what I was stitching and it ripped right off when I was done.

B. Tissue paper or wax paper also works well, but neither one has the benefit of being transparent.

C. If you are working on a single-sided project, you can avoid the problem altogether by sewing on the less-sticky wrong side of the fabric.

D. You also avoid the problem when you are sewing rick-rack or other trim onto your oilcloth or vinyl. Let's hear it for rick-rack!

E. Putting some clear tape on the bottom of your presser foot will also help with the drag. Just be sure to leave a short tail of tape coming off the back of the foot for easy removal later.

F. A roller foot with little wheels built in glides over vinyl much more easily than a regular presser foot can—you can order one to fit your machine from the manufacturer or most large sewing machine repair shops.

2. Always use a heavier needle made for sewing on leather, vinyl, or denim.

3. Use decorative scissors to create a fancy edge on your vinyl seams. This way you can create a neat and unusual look while leaving your seams on the outside.

4. Leave about a 1-inch border of extra vinyl around the edges of your sewing projects. When you are finished, you can trim these edges off with scissors. Leaving this extra vinyl gives you room for error in case it shifts while you are sewing, and you don't need to worry about lining up your seams.

5. Create unusual projects (like the Coloring Book Tote on page 235) by placing images between two layers of clear or tinted vinyl. An easy way to do this is to start with one larger piece of vinyl and fold it in half with your image between the two layers. (See Fig. 1.) This way you are dealing with just one piece of fabric, rather than two that might shift while sewing.

6. If you place an image between two layers of vinyl, make sure you clean the inside of the vinyl so you don't have lint or fingerprints showing on top of your image.

SUPERSTAR LUGGAGE TAG

BY TORIE

YOU'LL NEED

Star pattern (or pattern shape of your choice)

One piece of red vinyl, 5 inches square

Two pieces of blue vinyl, each 5-1/4 inches square

Red and blue thread

One piece of clear vinyl, 5-1/4 inches square

Two pieces of heavy card-stock, each 4-1/2 inches square

1/8-inch-wide red ribbon

TOOLS

Scissors

Tape measure

Fabric glue

Sewing machine

Hole punch

Pen or pencil

Unless your suitcase is neon green, it can be almost impossible to determine which one is yours as it rides around the carousel at the airport baggage claim terminal. There's nothing worse than standing by the conveyor belt after a long day of travel, watching all of those black and navy blue bags roll by and wondering when yours is going to come out . . . or if it already has, and someone else has grabbed it by mistake.

Put your super crafting powers to work and make your baggage easy to spot with a cute and funky vinyl luggage tag! Even if you don't have a big trip coming up, you can make a fun tag to spice up your everyday tote, your gym bag, or any other bag you carry on a regular basis.

1. Cut out the star pattern in cardstock. (See Fig. 1.) Trace this pattern in pen or pencil onto the back of the red vinyl piece.

2. To cut the star shape out of the red vinyl, leaving the outside edges of the vinyl intact, cut a small slit in the center of the star you traced. Now carefully cut out the star shape so that it becomes negative space and you're left with a piece of red vinyl with a star-shaped hole in the middle.

3. Trace the star shape onto the back of one of the pieces of blue vinyl.

4. You're going to cut a slightly larger star out this time, so cut ¼ inch outside of the traced lines. Follow the cutting instructions in step 2 to cut out the star shape, leaving the edges of the vinyl intact.

5. Align the two pieces of vinyl with the star cut-outs so that the right sides are facing up and the blue one is on top of the red one. You should be able to see the perimeter of the red star cut-out through the larger blue star cut-out. Put a little fabric glue near the edges between the two pieces to hold them together.

6. Topstitch along the perimeter of the star on the blue vinyl in red thread, ⅛ inch from the edge of the cut-out. This will hold the blue and red vinyl pieces together.

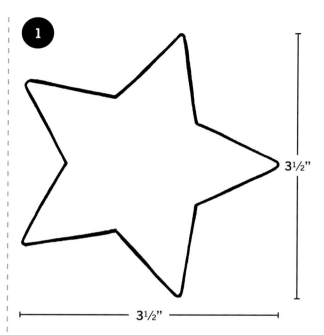

3½"

3½"

7. Place the piece of clear vinyl behind the piece you have just sewn together so that the edges of the blue and clear vinyl squares are lined up. Put a little fabric glue near the edges between these pieces to hold them together.

8. Determine which side of the square you would like to be the top. Topstitch in blue along this side, ⅛ inch from the edge. This will hold the clear vinyl in place once the luggage tag is finished so that your address will slide in behind the clear vinyl.

9. To attach the back of the luggage tag, take the other square of blue vinyl and align it, wrong sides together, with the layered square. Put a little fabric glue along the two sides and the bottom to hold the pieces together. Do not put glue along the top edge.

10. Topstitch in blue thread around the sides and bottom of the luggage tag to hold the front and back together, 1/8 inch from the edge. Leave the top open.

11. Punch two holes in the center of the open side, approximately 1/2 inch down from the top and 1/2 inch apart.

12. Write your address or whatever information you want to show on the cardstock. Slide the paper inside the luggage tag between the clear vinyl and the back piece.

13. Cut a 12- to 16-inch piece of ribbon.

14. Starting at the front of the luggage tag,

Experiment with different shapes and colors and use any leftover vinyl scraps to make Wonder Cuffs (page 55). Or buy enough of the same patterns of vinyl to make a matching set with the Gingham Delight Belt (page 233), luggage tag, and cuffs.

thread one end of the ribbon through one of the holes so that it comes out in the back. Then thread it from the back out through the other hole so that it comes out in the front. You should now have a ribbon loop at the back of the tag.

15. Place the ribbon loop under your luggage handle or wherever you would like to attach the tag. Holding the loop in place, pull the luggage tag up and over the handle and through the loop so that the ribbon is secured around the handle of the bag. Adjust the length as necessary and tie the ends of the ribbon into a secure bow at the front of your tag.

16. Bon voyage!

GINGHAM DELIGHT BELT

YOU'LL NEED

A belt that fits you well

1/8 yard black and white gingham oilcloth

Fabric glue

Iron-on alphabet letters that spell "handmade" (or the word of your choice)

Craft glue

Two 1-1/2-inch metal rings

TOOLS

Measuring tape

Scissors

Sewing pins

Sewing machine and black thread

Scrap paper

Toothpick

Declare to the world that you wear handmade with this cute retro-styled gingham belt.

1. Measure the length of a belt that fits you well and add 3 inches. Cut two strips of gingham oilcloth that are each 1½ inches wide and as long as the belt plus 3 inches measurement.

2. Apply fabric glue to the wrong side of one strip of oilcloth. Then press the two strips together, wrong sides facing, so the gingham shows on both sides. Add pins as necessary to hold the two strips together.

3. Stitch the belt pieces together along both long sides, ⅛ inch from the edge.

4. Take each of the iron-on letters that you will need to spell your word and determine where you would like them on the belt. Use the belt that fits you well as a reference to see how far from the buckle you will need to place the letters so that they are visible across your back when you put the belt on.

5. Put a dab of craft glue on some scrap paper. Using a toothpick, apply a thin coat of glue to the back of each iron-on letter and glue them onto the oilcloth belt, one at a time. Allow the glue to dry.

6. To attach the metal rings, take the left end of the belt and put it through both rings. Fold down 2 inches on the end of the oilcloth strip to the inside of the belt so that you have just created a loop to hold the rings in place. Pin the fold down and stitch a reinforced box approximately 1 inch wide to secure the rings inside the loop. (See Fig. 1.)

Use any extra oilcloth to make Wonder Cuffs (page 55), an Envelope Change Purse (page 239), or a Checkbook Cozy (page 241). Play around with adding grommets or other words and phrases to personalize your hand-made belt.

7. On the right end of the belt, fold the last ½ inch of the oilcloth strip to the inside of the belt. Pin it in place and stitch a straight line from the top edge to the bottom of the belt to hold the fold in place.

COLORING BOOK TOTE

BY CATHY

YOU'LL NEED

Two coloring book or magazine pages, 10 inches by 13 inches

Two pieces tinted vinyl, 12 inches by 28 inches (front and back of bag)

One piece tinted vinyl, 8 inches by 11-1/2 inches (bottom)

One piece of thicker cardboard with an interesting design, 6 inches by 10 inches (bottom of bag)

Two pieces oilcloth, 7 inches by 29 inches (sides)

Two pieces oilcloth, 2-1/2 inches by 22 inches (handles)

TOOLS

Scissors or pinking shears

Sewing machine with contrasting thread

1/4-inch hole punch

Grommet pliers

Four sets of 1/4-inch grommets

I have a thing for vintage imagery. My shelves are overflowing with the tattered books, magazines, advertisements, and coloring books I can't resist at estate sales and thrift stores. I feel as though I am preserving an ordinary piece of the past that could so easily otherwise be forgotten. This tinted vinyl tote is a great way to display and preserve the pages of a book or magazine that keep falling out but that you can't bear to throw away.

1. Fold the front vinyl piece in half, placing one coloring book page inside (See Fig. 1 in Vinyl 101 on page 226). The fold should be at the top of the picture. Leave a ¼-inch border between the fold and the top of the page. Sew all around the outside of the paper page, staying as close to its edge as you can. You will have a large border of excess vinyl on the sides and bottom. These will get trimmed off when you have completely assembled your bag. Repeat this step with the second coloring book page and the back vinyl piece.

2. Take the bottom vinyl piece and fold it in half, placing the cardboard piece inside. Sew around the edge as you did in step 1, but leave an equally large border on all four sides.

3. Fold the two oilcloth side pieces in half. The fold will go at the top of the bag. You are going to attach these two side pieces to the front and back pieces to assemble the body of your bag. The excess vinyl edges will remain on the outside of the bag and will be trimmed in the final step.

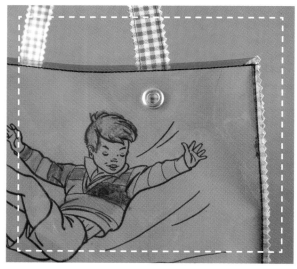

4. Start by stitching one side piece to the front piece with the wrong sides together. You will want to stitch along the seam that is already on the front piece from step 1. Using the same method, stitch the back piece onto the other edge of the oilcloth side piece. Finish off by sewing the second oilcloth side piece on, one edge to the front piece and one edge to the back piece. You should now have all four sides forming the body of a bag without a bottom.

5. Line the bottom piece up with the lower edges of the main part of the bag with wrong sides together. Stitch all around the edge of the bottom, attaching it to the bag.

6. Use pinking shears (or regular scissors) to neatly trim off all the excess vinyl edges. Trim to within about ¼ inch of the seam.

7. Take one of the oilcloth handle pieces and fold it in half lengthwise, right side out, so that you have one long thin piece. Stitch all around the edges of the oilcloth strip, sewing about ½ inch from the edge. Repeat with the second oilcloth handle piece. Use scissors or pinking shears to trim away the excess oilcloth from the long edges of both handles.

You can adjust the size of your vinyl pieces if you want to use a smaller image to make a smaller tote. Just be sure to leave about 1 inch of excess vinyl around the edges, then trim them off once your bag is completely assembled.

8. Mark two spots on both the front and back of the bag where the handles will go, about ¾ inch from the top and 2½ inches from each side seam. Use the hole punch to make these four holes. Also punch holes about ½ inch from each end of both handles.

9. Take one handle and use the grommet pliers and grommets to attach its holes to both holes on the bag front (the handle ends should go on the inside of the bag). Repeat this step with the second handle on the back of the bag. Refer to the directions on your grommet pliers for specifics on how to attach grommets.

ENVELOPE CHANGE PURSE

CHECKBOOK COZY

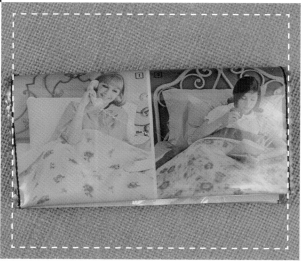

ENVELOPE CHANGE PURSE + CHECKBOOK COZY

YOU'LL NEED

Paper image, 10 inches tall by 5 inches wide (use comics, old advertising, wrapping paper, or even fabric)

Clear or tinted vinyl piece, 12 inches square

TOOLS

Scissors, plain or decorative

Sewing machine and thread

1/4-inch hole punch

Snap pliers and one snap

I love vintage packaging and advertisements and am always looking for ways to use them in my art. You can create fun and functional things like this cute change purse and checkbook cover by preserving cool vintage imagery between two layers of clear vinyl.

ENVELOPE CHANGE PURSE

1. Refer to Fig. 1 for tips on arranging your image so that all sides will be right side up when the purse is assembled.

2. Round the corners on one of the short ends of your paper image. This will be the front flap of your purse.

3. Take the vinyl piece and fold it in half widthwise. Place the image in the vinyl fold, making sure it is centered. You should have roughly a 1-inch border of vinyl left on all sides.

4. Carefully sew all around the image, getting as close as you can to the edge. Refer to Vinyl 101 on page 226 for helpful hints on sewing with vinyl.

1

STAMPS

5. Trim off the excess vinyl, cutting close to the sewn edge. If you are using decorative scissors, you will want to wait until step 7 so that the edges will line up.

6. Hold your trimmed piece face down with the rounded edge at the top. Fold the bottom edge up about 4 inches. This is the body of your purse. Sew up the two side seams, reinforcing the top with backstitching so that it doesn't tear with use.

7. If you are using decorative scissors, you can trim the excess vinyl from the edges and top now.

8. Fold down the top flap. Use the hole punch to make a hole on both the top flap and the body of the purse, lining them up so the two snap pieces will meet. Following the instructions on the package of snaps, use your snap pliers to attach both sides of the snap to the purse. If you don't have snap pliers, you can make a buttonhole and use a button.

9. This purse can be made in any size you want. Make it larger for an art portfolio or longer for a pencil case.

CHECKBOOK COZY

1. Remember to arrange your images so that when the cover is folded in half, both images will be right side up. Place your paper image between the two layers of vinyl. Carefully stitch around the edges of the image. If you are using two separate images for the front and back of the cover, you will need to stitch a seam between them to hold them in place.

2. Use plain scissors to trim the excess vinyl from the two short ends. Cut close to the stitching, leaving only about a ⅛ inch border.

3. Lay the image right side down and fold both short ends up 2¾ inches toward the center. These will be the pockets that you insert your

YOU'LL NEED

Paper image, 12 inches tall by 6-1/8 inches wide (use comics, old advertising, wrapping paper, or even fabric)

Two clear or tinted vinyl pieces, 13 inches tall by 7-1/8 inches wide

TOOLS

Sewing machine and thread

Scissors

Decorative scissors or pinking shears (optional)

I scanned my images into the computer and flipped part of it so that when I folded it over to form the purse, it wasn't upside down (as in Fig. 1). If you don't have a scanner you can manually cut and paste, which is what I did with the checkbook cozy.

The paper between the vinyl layers is going to get some wear and tear, so use a thinner paper that will bend without creasing and wrinkling too much.

You can buy clear or tinted vinyl at most fabric stores for only $3–$4 per yard. The clear vinyl comes in several thicknesses, while the tinted comes in a variety of cool translucent colors like pink, green, yellow, and blue.

checkbook and check register into. Stitch up each side of the pocket, reinforcing the tops with backstitching so that they don't rip with wear. Repeat with the second pocket.

4. Using decorative scissors or pinking shears, trim the excess vinyl from both sides of the cover. If you don't want to be fancy, you can use plain old scissors.

5. Fold the entire thing in half so that the pockets are on the inside, and you're done!

PDX KNITTING NEEDLE ORGANIZER

BY SUSAN

YOU'LL NEED

A clean and dry coffee can (mine measured 9 inches tall and 16 inches around)

Paper towel rolls (I used six)

Art paper of your choice

Glue stick

Ribbon (I used 1/2-inch-wide red grosgrain)

Craft glue

Extra-wide double-fold bias tape

TOOLS

Sharp knife (for nonmetal can)

Scissors

Measuring tape or ruler

This project combines three things I love about living in Portland: coffee, recycling, and knitting. I made mine using color-copied 1940s fabric for a design reminiscent of a vintage hatbox, but you can use different papers and ribbon combinations to make yours as modern as you like.

If you go through coffee cans as fast as I do, you'll be making these for every knitter you know. You can also make a shorter version to organize your crochet hooks and double-pointed needles.

1. Remove the coffee can label. If there is a lip or metal top on a cardboard coffee can, use a sharp knife to carefully saw off the top of the can. If you are using a metal can, leave it intact.

2. If your paper towel rolls are taller than the can, use your sharp knife or scissors to cut them down so they are slightly shorter than the can's height. Set them aside.

3. Measure your can and cut the art paper to size so that it covers the can, overlapping slightly along a vertical side seam. Use the glue stick to coat the outside of the can evenly with glue. Press the paper onto the can, smoothing it down so there are no air bubbles.

4. Cover the side seam with ribbon, using craft glue to adhere it. If you'd like to, add another strip of ribbon to the opposite side and trim the bottom edge of the organizer with ribbon for a finished look.

5. Cut a piece of bias tape just slightly longer than the can's circumference and use craft glue to glue it over the top edge of the can, overlapping the bias tape at the side seam.

SAN FRANCISCO CROCHET HOOK ORGANIZER

Follow the directions for the needle organizer, but cut the can down to 4 inches tall and use toilet paper tubes instead of paper towel rolls.

For even more knitting needle organization excitement, try making the Knit-It! Bag (page 43), which features handy vertical pockets in every size.

6. Place your paper towel rolls into the can, cut sides down, until they are wedged in. Each roll can hold a different size of needles (or a range of sizes).

7. Never lose your 7s again!

YOU'LL NEED

Clean and dry glass jar

Glue stick

Tissue paper cut into 1/2- to 1-inch squares (I used five colors)

Decoupage medium

Glitter (optional)

Water-based sealant (optional)

Ribbon (I used 3/8-inch-wide blue grosgrain)

Craft glue

TOOLS

Paintbrush

Scissors

GLOWING GLASS CANDLEHOLDER

This easy project converts a plain glass jar into a gorgeously glossy candleholder. Decoupaging tissue paper squares in three layers makes the colors glow like a stained-glass window!

1. Apply a thin layer of glue from the glue stick all over the area of the jar you want to cover. Place squares of tissue paper in random color combinations over the glass, smoothing them down to stick to the jar. Add more glue if necessary.

2. Apply a coat of decoupage medium to the first layer of paper. (I mixed some glitter into mine for a sparkling effect.) Use your paintbrush to cover the tissue paper evenly. Don't worry if the paper wrinkles!

3. Add another layer of tissue paper over the first, adhering it with more decoupage medium, and cover it with another coat.

4. Add a third layer of paper squares the same way and cover it with a final coat of decoupage medium.

5. After it has dried, apply a coat of sealant (or, if you like, use one last layer of medium instead). Let it sit overnight.

6. Cut two pieces of ribbon the circumference of the jar and glue them on with craft glue to define the edges of the design and cover any uneven spots.

7. Place a votive candle inside and enjoy your new candleholder!

Note: Be careful not to leave tissue paper anywhere near the candle's flame! Leave a space at the top of the jar with no paper attached (as shown in the photograph).

MINI BACK MASSAGER

YOU'LL NEED

One small paint roller

One empty thread spool (size will depend on the size of the paint roller handle)

Craft glue

Glitter

Decorative paper scraps

Clear shelf paper or clear tape

TOOLS

Newspaper

Scissors

Hole punch

Wouldn't a back massage be nice right about now? You don't need to spend tons of money on an expensive back massager when you can easily make your own. Chances are good that you probably have a lot of the materials around the house, too!

1. Take the roller sponge off the roller so you have a handle with an empty bar. Sometimes there is a cylindrical piece of plastic under the roller that you'll also need to pull off the bar so the spool will fit. If the handle has a cap that fits on the end of the bar, set it aside. You'll need it to keep the spool on the bar. If it doesn't have one, find some sort of end cap that will fit on the end of the bar. (Your chance to be extra creative!)

2. If the roller handle that you have is round and adding glitter to it would make it impractical, skip to step 7. If your handle is flat and indented on each side, continue with step 3.

3. Spread newspaper over your workspace. Fill one side of the roller handle with glue and then sprinkle glitter generously over it so all of the glue is covered. Allow it to dry.

4. Pick up the handle and gently shake off the excess glitter. Turn the handle over and repeat step 3 on the other side.

5. Once it's dry, shake off the excess glitter.

6. If desired, cover the cap that fits on the end of the bar with glue and then sprinkle glitter over it. It may take a few phases of gluing and glittering to cover the entire cap. Allow it to dry, and then shake off the excess glitter. This step is especially helpful if the cap you're using doesn't match the original roller handle.

7. To decorate the spool, cut a piece of paper large enough to wrap around the middle of the spool where the thread used to be. Cut a piece of shelf paper or clear tape of the same size.

8. Glue the strip of paper onto the center of the spool. Then cover the paper with the piece of shelf paper or clear tape.

9. Cut two circles out of the decorative paper large enough to cover the ends of the spool. (If the spool still has the stickers on the ends, use one of those as a template.)

10. Determine where the center of each paper circle is and punch a hole using your hole punch. Glue the paper circles onto each end of the spool.

11. Place the spool on the roller bar, put the cap on the end, and you're ready for a massage!

LUMINOUS TIN FLOWERS

YOU'LL NEED

Cardstock for template

Brightly colored soda cans (two cans will make three double-layered flowers)

TOOLS

Scissors

Pencil

1/4-inch hole punch

Flat-nose pliers or grommet pliers and three sets of grommets

The bright vintage foil reflectors on 1950s and '60s Christmas lights inspired these recycled beauties. Get yourself a silver aluminum tree and a light-up color wheel, and you're set!

1. Use the shapes in Fig. 1 to make a template out of cardstock. (Feel free to come up with your own designs!)

2. Use your scissors to cut the top and bottom off the soda cans. Cut down the center of the cylinder that is left to make a large flat piece of metal.

3. Use a pencil to trace the shapes onto the soda cans. Trace them onto the front side so that you can see what colors and designs will be on your flowers.

4. Cut the shapes out with scissors. The metal is sharp and will tear easily, so be very careful.

1

2"

3¼"

2"

3½"

Remember to be careful when cutting soda cans. They can be very sharp and can leave small slivers of metal. I used fruit nectar cans. Their fantastic colorful images are great for the flowers.

If you want your flowers to fit over Christmas lights, you will need to use ⅜-inch grommets and compatible grommet pliers.

These flowers can be used for much more than just Christmas lights. Nail them to a wooden frame, embellish a boring lampshade, brighten a room by adding them to a plain curtain rod . . . use your imagination!

5. Punch holes in the centers of the flowers. If the hole punch won't reach, use scissors to carefully make a ¼-inch hole.

6. Mix and match colors to create contrasting combinations of small and large flowers.

7. Use a grommet to attach the small flower to the center of the large one. Secure it with the grommet pliers. If you don't have grommet pliers, you can also use flat-nose pliers to bend the metal around the inside of the holes towards the back to hold them in place.

SPARKLING MAGIC WAND

BY TORIE

YOU'LL NEED

Paper towel roll

Scraps of newspaper

Piece of 12-inch by
12-inch paper

Decoupage medium

Craft glue

Lightweight cardboard
(like a pasta box)

Yellow acrylic paint

Glitter

1/4 yard tulle

TOOLS

Scissors

String or rubber band

Pencil

Two sponge (or plain)
paintbrushes

A glittery magic wand would make a great gift for a youngster . . . or anyone you know who likes hocus-pocus!

1. Cut the paper towel roll open vertically so that it is a rectangle instead of a tube. Roll it up as tightly as you can and glue the top flap down so you now have a smaller tube than before. Secure it with string tied around it or hold it closed with a rubber band until the glue dries.

2. Cover your work area with scrap newspaper. Take your 12-inch square piece of paper and apply decoupage medium to the back of it with a sponge brush. Center your paper towel roll on one corner of the paper and roll it up in the paper diagonally so the entire tube is covered, wrapping it several times. Glue down the top and bottom ends as needed, or tuck the excess paper into the tube.

3. Cut two star shapes from Fig. 1 on page 230 out of lightweight cardboard (the wand uses the same star pattern as the luggage tag). Paint the stars yellow. Allow them to dry. Put on as many coats of yellow paint as needed to adequately cover the cardboard. On the last coat, while it is wet still, sprinkle some glitter over the stars.

4. Rip small pieces of newspaper to cover the handle of the wand. Put some decoupage medium on the back of each piece of newspaper and stick them on the wand. Once it is covered as much as you'd like, put one coat of the medium over the top of the entire handle. While the handle is still wet, sprinkle glitter over it. (You may want to do this in a few rounds: Decoupage and glitter one section, allow them to dry, and then move on to another section).

See what other kinds of recycled materials you can incorporate into a wand!

5. Glue the bottom one-third of each star onto the top end of your wand so the stars are back to back. Don't glue the stars together—there should be a gap between them.

6. Take the tulle and gather it in the middle so it is a little bunched up. Then glue the center of the bunch to the back of each star, above the end of the wand.

7. Abracadabra! You're done!

FINISHING TOUCHES

LABELS + PACKAGING 101

A personalized tag or label is the perfect finishing touch to make your handmade project special. You don't need to buy premade gift tags or labels. Making your own is quite easy. Here are a few tips:

1. Invest in Photoshop and a decent scanner. You can scan and collage together your own images to create personalized packaging, business cards, and product labels. Instead of purchasing clip art, you can create your own by scanning old copyright-free books and magazines.

2. Buy a paper cutter. You can print out pages of multiple tags and cut them out neatly and quickly with your cutter. They come in several sizes, so you can choose the one that best fits your needs. The smaller size is portable and works for smaller volume jobs, while the larger one can cut several thicknesses and has a ruler guide attached.

3. You can have a rubber stamp made of any black and white image. Check your area for an office supply or stamp store that will do this for you.

4. Paper punches are available in a variety of sizes and shapes. Use these to make your tags, labels, or even business cards.

5. Use vintage playing cards, tarot cards, and recipe cards to make your own tags.

6. Decorate tins, matchboxes, and film canisters to create recycled packaging for small items. See Found-Object Packaging on page 271.

7. Including a tag with information about yourself on your item will encourage people to appreciate that it is handmade. Whether it is a gift or for sale, a personalized label lets people know that the item is not mass-produced, but is handmade and one of a kind.

8. You can buy packages of full-sheet adhesive paper at most office supply stores. Use your computer to lay out whole sheets of stickers and cut them with your rotary cutter.

9. You can also buy packages of stickers in various sizes—circles, squares, and rectangles. Some brands even offer templates that you can download off their websites and plug your graphics into for easy sticker making!

10. Translucent plastic or polyethylene bags are a good way to package handmade soap and jewelry. Tie it off with a little ribbon for a quick and easy gift package.

11. You can use decoupage techniques (page 264) to decorate labels or gift cards, as well as design bigger pieces.

There are amazing online resources where you can have stickers or postcards made, find cool clip art, and order custom fabric labels. See **www.pdxsupercrafty.com** for an ever-changing list of our personal favorites.

CARDS GALORE!

FOR ONE CARD YOU'LL NEED

One piece of 8-1/2-inch by 11-inch cardstock

A fun image from newspapers, magazines, or even personal photos

A background piece like wallpaper, foil, or fabric

Fun accents to add like sewing trim, buttons, old labels

Glue stick or double-sided tape

Thread in contrasting colors

TOOLS

Scissors or pinking shears

Sewing machine or needle and thread

BOWL-O-RAMA + KITCHEN QUEEN STITCHED CARDS

This project is a cool alternative to the usual decoupage-style collage. The great thing about sewing on paper is that you are not necessarily sewing to hold pieces together, but for decoration! Be creative and sew shapes or designs on your card—you don't have to stick to sewing around the edges. Use this method to make your own cards, gift tags, or invitations.

1. Start by folding your cardstock in half widthwise and decide what size you want your card to be. You want to create a layered look by having the items sized so that they all show when placed on top of each other. Experiment with the image and the background to determine what size cardstock will best frame

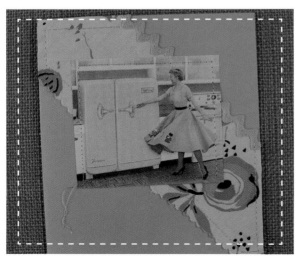

your project. Use pinking shears or regular scissors to trim the cardstock.

2. Lightly tack your different items onto the cardstock using a glue stick or double-sided tape. This will keep them in place while you are sewing. You can glue them all on and just stitch once around the edges, or sew them on one at a time to create a more layered look.

3. I like to leave a small tail of thread hanging from the beginning and end of the sewing. This keeps the stitching from coming undone, and looks pretty cool, too. If you don't have a sewing machine, you can hand-stitch or embroider your different elements.

A bone folder is a great tool to have on hand. You can use it to smooth down the folds when working with paper.

You can even sew an envelope by folding a piece of paper and cutting it so it is slightly larger than the card. Sew around three sides to create a kind of pocket for your card.

CUPCAKE + DJ CRAFTY CARDS

1. Make a neat crease to fold the cardstock in half so it measures 5½ inches across by 4¼ inches tall.

2. Use the patterns in Figs. 1 and 2 to cut out the shapes for the cupcake or record player in the colors of your choice.

3. For all cards, apply a thin coat of glue on the back of the first shape with the glue stick. Glue it to your card, smoothing it flat with your fingertips or the side of a pencil.

FOR ONE CARD YOU'LL NEED

One 8-1/2-inch by 5-1/2-inch piece of cardstock (cut an 8-1/2-inch by 11-inch sheet in half if you want to make two cards)

Brightly colored art paper or origami paper

Glue stick

Decoupage medium

Glitter (optional)

TOOLS

Scissors

Pen

Small paintbrush

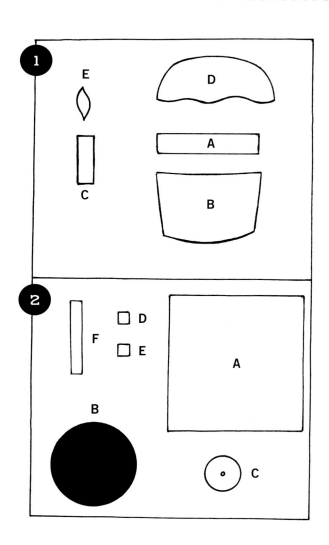

Repeat with the other shapes, in the order listed below for each one.

• For the cupcake, glue the sliver of cake showing (see Fig. 1A) as the first layer and end with the candle flame (see Fig. 1E).

• For the record player, start with the background piece (see Fig. 2A) and finish with the record player arm (see Fig. 2F). With a pen, draw a dot in the center of the record.

4. Use a small paintbrush to apply a thin layer of decoupage medium over the entire surface of the card. Smooth the pieces down with the paintbrush if air bubbles or creases develop. Let it dry completely. Add a second coat to seal the card. If you like, mix a little glitter into the decoupage medium to create a sparkling surface, as shown in the cupcake card photograph.

LOVE ATTACK BLOCK PRINT CARD

YOU'LL NEED

Vintage or new anatomical image of the heart (or image of your choice)

Carbon paper (optional)

Smooth and thick watercolor paper

Plastic wrap

Vintage or new trim

Craft glue

TOOLS

Rubber block print, square or rectangle

Hand carver with thin and thick carver attachments

Block print ink

Block print roller

Ball-point pen

Tape

Tin tray

Anatomical images of the human heart are endlessly fascinating and seem to show up in artwork across all cultures. I've become sort of obsessed with collecting vintage anatomical renderings of the human heart. While some may shy away from the heart and all of its veins, ventricles, and, of course, its tremendous aorta, I embrace this imagery and find it completely romantic. The Love Attack Block Print Card=Pure Romance. Make your own love card for someone special.

1. Choose an image online or from a book or magazine to use for your block print.

2. Purchase a block print square from your local art supply store. Beginners should use the soft rubber type that is easy to carve.

3. Pick out a carver and buy at least two carver tips: one small one to carve fine lines, and one large one to carve thick lines.

4. Choose at least one color of block print ink and an ink roller. Sometimes art stores will sell a starter kit with a roller and block print carvers. I recommend choosing a few colors of block print ink to add more variety to the cards you will make for this project.

5. If you don't feel comfortable drawing freehand, buy carbon paper.

6. Choose a thick, smooth watercolor paper. If you don't own a paper cutter, ask the art supply store to cut down your watercolor paper,

or you can pay a visit to your local copy store and use their cutter on the sly.

7. Draw your image with ball-point pen on the block print square. For nonfreehand card-makers, tape the carbon paper with the carbon side down on your square. Tape your image on top of the carbon paper and carefully trace over the image using a ball-point pen. The carbon will transfer the image onto your square.

8. Carve the lines of your image using your block print carver. Use both types of carvers to achieve both thin and thick lines.

9. Cover a 10-inch by 10-inch space on your table with plastic wrap.

10. Tape down a piece of watercolor paper.

11. Squeeze a teaspoon-size amount of block print ink into your tin tray. You can also experiment by mixing colors.

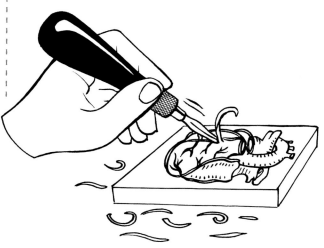

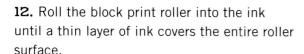

12. Roll the block print roller into the ink until a thin layer of ink covers the entire roller surface.

13. Roll a thin layer of ink over your block print square.

14. Pick up the block print square and place it firmly on the watercolor paper. Lightly press the block into the paper. With one hand, hold down the paper as you slowly pull the block off your paper with the other hand.

15. Check out your cool block print!

16. Repeat steps 14–15, re-inking the roller as needed, until you have made your desired number of cards. (If you want to try another color, rinse and hand dry the block and the tin.)

17. Let the cards dry for 30 minutes.

18. Frame with vintage or new trim as desired.

19. Give the cards to special people in your life!

TEN-MINUTE CARD

It's always handy to stock extra cards in case a special occasion sneaks up on you. If you get caught short, here's a quick and easy one that you can make in less than 10 minutes.

1. Pull your silk flowers off the stems. Take out whatever is in the center of the flower so you have a place to glue the rhinestone. Glue one rhinestone in the center of each flower using your craft glue. Allow the glue to set while you're cutting out the rest of the card.

2. Cut a 5½-inch by 8½-inch piece of green cardstock. Fold it in half so that you have a 5½-inch by 4¼ -inch card.

3. Cut a 5-inch by 3¾ -inch piece of pink cardstock. Then cut that rectangle into diagonal strips, each approximately ½-inch to ¾-inch wide. It looks very cool if they're all a little different in width.

4. Take four of the pink strips (or more if you like) and place them across the front of the green card, starting in the center. Space them approximately ¼-inch apart, leaving room in the bottom left- and upper right-hand corners for the silk flowers. Glue the strips into place using your glue stick.

5. To glue the silk flowers in place, put a little dab of craft glue on the back of the flower and place it on the card. Hold it in place for a few seconds so the glue can set. Glue three flowers in a triangle on the bottom left-hand corner and two flowers side by side in the upper right-hand corner. (Or you can play around with where you want the flowers to be before you glue them to create your own design.)

6. Let the card dry for about an hour before placing it in an envelope.

YOU'LL NEED

Five tiny white silk flowers (or more if you like)

Rhinestones

Craft glue

Green and pink cardstock

Glue stick

TOOLS

Scissors or small paper cutter

Ruler

TEN-MINUTE CARD

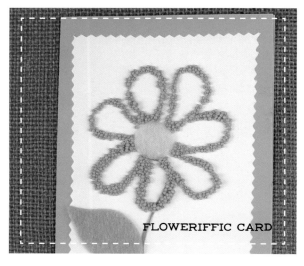

FLOWERIFFIC CARD

FLOWERIFFIC CARD

I love sitting on the floor with my cardstock and beads spread out in front of me. I usually don't know what I'm going to make until I've already started. This is how the flower card was born. Granted, I ended up with beads all over the floor, but I had fun in the process!

1. Fold a 7-inch by 8½-inch piece of cardstock in color #1 in half so you end up with a 7-inch by 4½-inch card.

2. Cut a 3¾-inch by 7½-inch piece of cardstock in color #2 with your pinking shears.

3. Glue the pinked paper to the front of the card, centered.

4. Cut a circle out of the felt that will be the center of the flower. The one shown here is ¾-inch in diameter. Glue the felt circle to the card (either centered, or slightly off-centered, it's up to you!) so that the top of the circle is approximately 1¾ inch from the top of the pinked paper.

BY TORIE

YOU'LL NEED

Cardstock (two colors)

Craft glue

Felt (two colors)

Sewing thread

Seed beads (color of your choice)

TOOLS

Scissors (regular and pinking shears)

Ruler

Pencil

Small bowl

5. Cut five pieces of sewing thread, each 5 inches long. Roll them together with your fingers so they wrap around each other a little, and glue them to the page where you would like the flower stem to be.

6. Draw the flower petals lightly around the felt circle with your pencil. You can draw as many or as few as you like.

7. To attach the beads, trace one petal with your glue. The more glue you put, the thicker your petals will look when covered with beads.

8. Before the glue has time to dry, sprinkle your seed beads generously over it so that it is well covered. Hold the card over a small bowl and gently tap the back so that the extra beads fall into the bowl. Use your fingernail to push stray beads into the petal formation or slightly reshape the petals as needed.

9. Repeat steps 7 and 8 for each petal.

10. Cut a leaf shape out of your other color of felt and glue it onto your flower card.

Try making different types of flowers and experimenting with different shapes cut out of felt, bordered by beads. Circles are an easy one to start with, and the cards can be as simple or as elaborate as you like!

WRAPPING IT UP

BOX IDEAS

Matchboxes

Cigar boxes

Card or stationery boxes

Candy tins

Office supply boxes

Cosmetic boxes

Plastic pin boxes

RIBBON IDEAS

Old sewing trim: rick-rack, bias tape, lace, sequins, etc.

Embroidery thread

An old fabric measuring tape

Pipe cleaners

Fabric cut into strips with pinking shears

EXTRAS

Fake flowers or fruit

Buttons

Little toys

Charms

Cake toppers

Holiday ornaments

GIFT TAG IDEAS

Cut up . . .

Old greeting cards

Advertising

Comics

Cereal boxes

Sheet music

Office labels

Found photographs

FOUND-OBJECT PACKAGING

I have always felt that the packaging of a gift is just as important as what's inside. In fact, I like to make the packaging a sort of bonus present as well. By using everyday found objects, you can create one-of-a-kind packaging for your gifts while also cutting down on the major waste of conventional wrapping paper. The supplies you need for this kind of packaging are readily available and super cheap at thrift stores and estate sales. You might even have some stashed in your basement. Below are some ideas to start you off, but with a little creativity I'm sure you can come up with an endless list of found-object packaging supplies.

FOUND OBJECT

CANDY WRAPPER

FLOWER

WRAPPING WITH SCARVES

Vintage scarves aplenty can be found in thrift stores. Why not make the gift wrap a part of the gift as well? Snatch up the pretty ones when you find them and you'll always have plenty of wrapping supplies on hand.

YOU'LL NEED

A gift that needs wrapping

Gift box

Vintage scarf

Ribbon

Tape

TRADITIONAL BOW
BEST WITH A LONG, NARROW SCARF

1. Center the gift box on top of the wrong side of the scarf.

2. Bring the long ends of the scarf up around the top of the box and tie a bow just as you would tie a ribbon.

CANDY WRAPPER

1. Center the box on one edge of the wrong side of the scarf.

2. Hold or tape the edge of the scarf to the box, then roll the box so that it's wrapped in the scarf. Continue rolling it until you reach the other end. Put a small piece of tape under the edge to hold.

3. Cut two pieces of ribbon. Tie them around the scarf at each end of the box.

FLOWER

1. Follow steps 1 and 2 of the Candy Wrapper instructions.

2. Take the two loose ends of the scarf and pull them up to the top of the box.

3. Twist those ends around each other in a swirling pattern until you have a flower. Tuck the ends in and tape as necessary.

PERSONALIZING
EMBROIDERY 101

Hand embroidering is the perfect way to personalize a gift, appliqué, or keepsake. You can stitch words or initials, or design a gorgeous image or pattern . . . the possibilities are infinite! There are hundreds of embroidery stitches, but the projects in this book use three basic ones.

RUNNING STITCH

We also talked about this one in Sewing 101 on page 22. Simply weave the point of the needle in and out of the fabric, always sewing forward. Use longer stitches on the top of the fabric to form the design, and shorter stitches in between to anchor them on the back. This works well for embroidering words, as seen in the "Knit It!" appliqués (page 41).

CHAIN STITCH

This stitch creates a thicker line of small looped stitches rather than the broken-line look of the running stitch. Start by bringing your needle up from behind the fabric and pull your thread all the way through so you have a long piece to work with. Insert the needle back in the same spot (see Fig. 2A) and bring it out again slightly ahead as if you're making a running stitch (see Fig. 2B), but catch the loose thread loop under the needle's point before you pull the stitch all the way through. Repeat to

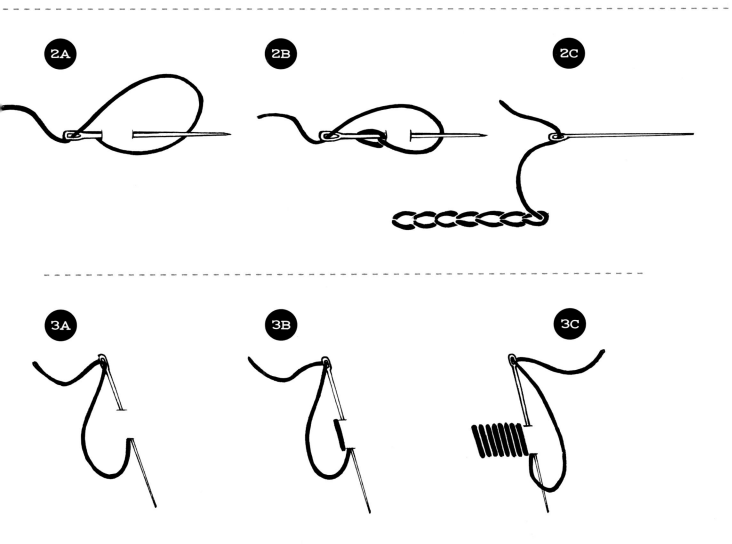

form a chain of stitches (see Fig. 2C). This is a great textured stitch for curved lines.

SATIN STITCH

This stitch fills up bigger spaces with even rows of vertical or horizontal straight-line stitching. You'll start with one stitch, sewing up from bottom to top (see Fig. 3A). Then make another parallel vertical stitch right next to it to fill in the design (see Fig. 3B). Continue stitching close together to fill in your space (see Fig. 3C). In this version, the back of your embroidery will look just like the front—you are filling in both sides, essentially. You'll use the satin stitch the same way you would use a marker on paper, to evenly fill in a space with parallel lines.

ASTERISK

An asterisk is perfect to punctuate an exclamation point or dot an *i*, or as a starry design element in your stitching. To make a six-point asterisk, just fol-low the steps in Figs. 4. First, make a vertical stitch (see Fig. 4A). Bring your needle out to the top right corner and make a diagonal stitch to the lower left corner (see Fig. 4B). Now bring your needle out on the lower right corner and make another diagonal stitch (see Fig. 4C). Once you complete your six-point asterisk (see Fig. 4D), secure the middle with a tiny stitch (see Fig. 4E).

TIPS

All fabrics are not created equal! Felt and woven

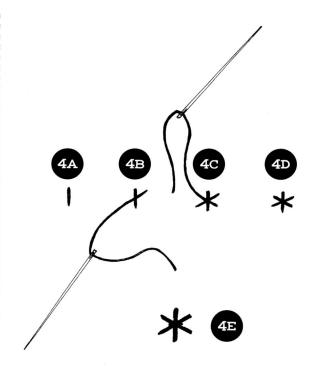

fabrics like denim, cotton broadcloth, and cordu-roy are wonderful to embroider on. Knit fabrics are not—they stretch and buckle and distort your stitches. So, if you want to embroider a shirt, a button-up or Western-style shirt will work really well, but a T-shirt may not. How about embroidering directly on an appliqué or patch, and sewing that to the T-shirt instead?

Use an adjustable embroidery hoop to keep your fabric neat and taut while you stitch on it.

The patterns in this book call for freehand transferring, using a water-soluble fabric pen. Draw your desired pattern on the fabric, using lines or solid color to indicate where the stitches will go. If you make a mistake, simply put a few drops of water on the design to erase it. You can use this method to create text, outlines, solid shapes, or anything else you dream up!

If you're using six-strand embroidery floss, you can pull one or two threads out to stitch with fairly easily if you cut it off at 36 inches (any longer, and it tangles quickly). Just grasp the one strand you want in one hand, and gently tug the others down the entire length. If you want two strands, pull them out one at a time.

Our recommended embroidery and needlework books are listed in Resources on page 279.

GIFT PACKS

Here are some handmade gift combinations that we recommend.

FOR YOUR CRAFTY FRIEND'S BIRTHDAY:
Knit It! Bag (page 43)
Emergency Craft Kit—Crafts to the Rescue! (page 119)
Cupcake Card (page 263)

FOR A KID'S BIRTHDAY:
Super Sock Monkey (page 27)
Sparkling Magic Wand (page 257)
Ten-Minute Card (page 267)

FOR A BRIDAL SHOWER:
A pair of pasties for the bride! (pages 58–64)
Aromatherapy Massage Oil (page 114)
Mini Back Massager (page 251)
-or-
Wonder Cuffs (page 55)
Superhero Slip + Boxers (page 143)

FOR A WEDDING:
Viva Oilcloth Placemats + Coasters (page 87)
Whale of a Pillow (page 91)
Love Attack Block Print Card (page 265)

RESOURCES

We've put together a short list of some of our favorite books, websites, and shops.

Check local thrift stores, estate sales, and garage sales for craft supplies and remarkable vintage objects just begging to be repurposed. Secondhand shopping yields amazing materials. Hardware and art supply stores are also great for craft shopping.

See more recommendations and links online at **www.pdxsupercrafty.com**

P.S. Buy handmade!

GENERAL CRAFTS

BUST magazine (**www.bust.com**) includes super cool craft projects and ideas in every issue.

Budget Living (**www.budgetliving.com**) mixes great affordable retro-modern decorating with projects to try at home.

www.craftster.org has thousands of inspiring projects contributed from crafters around the world.

Jen Bonnell's *DIY Girl* has excellent projects for the teenage craftista.

For a great selection of basic art supplies, including shrink plastic, glitter, and paper, check out **www.discountschoolsupply.com**.

Jean Railla's *Get Crafty* offers a spectrum of craft projects as well as fascinating narrative on radical homemaking. Her companion site, **www.getcrafty.com**, offers more how-to articles and crafty advice forums.

We love *Martha Stewart Living* (**www.marthastewart.com**) . . . what can we say, Martha rocks!

ReadyMade magazine (**www.readymademag.com**) combines very cool modern craft projects with features on creative living.

www.supernaturale.com offers craft articles and forums, too.

Venus (**www.venuszine.com**) has a great DIY section with inspiring how-tos and profiles of crafters and independent shops.

SEWING

Reader's Digest Complete Guide to Sewing is an incredible sewing book that covers everything you need to know from A–Z.

With its three-ring binder format, *Better Homes and Gardens Sewing Book* is a timeless classic. Used copies are readily available at bookshops and thrift stores.

www.reprodepotfabrics.com is an incredible site offering an unusual selection of vintage-inspired fabric and notions.

KNITTING

Debbie Stoller's *Stitch + Bitch* is an amazing knitting book for beginners and experienced knitters alike—it's clear and detailed, and includes forty fresh patterns. Her sequel, *Stitch + Bitch Nation*, has fifty incredible patterns, too!

Vicki Square's *Knitter's Companion* is a handy portable flip-guide to stitches and techniques.

www.knitty.com is a super cool online quarterly knitting mag.

www.about.com has knitting animation videos, which are much easier to follow than diagrams. Check one out if you get stuck!

www.learntoknit.com also has instructions, a FAQ page, links, and a forum to post questions or get advice.

EMBROIDERY, ETC.

Jenny Hart's *Stitch-It Kit* is wonderful—so is her site, **www.sublimestitching.com**.

The Good Housekeeping Illustrated Book of Needlecrafts is marvelous—it covers embroidery, appliqué, knitting, crocheting, and more.

We also love **www.subversivecrossstitch.com** for irreverent and cool cross-stitching designs.

JEWELRYMAKING

Rio Grande is a huge, comprehensive online and paper catalog for jewelrymaking supplies—**www.riogrande.com**.

www.firemountaingems.com has a gigantic online store of beads, jewelry tools, and findings. They send out a massive paper catalog once a year and supplemental catalogs every few months.

SHRINES

Kathy Cano-Murillo's *Making Shadow Boxes and Shrines* is a lovely and inspiring guide—don't miss her other books and her website, **www.craftychica.com**.

For an ever-changing variety of unique new and vintage pieces for your artwork, go to **www.silvercrowcreations.com**.

www.artchixstudio.com offers paper ephemera as well as other odds and ends for shrine-making and collage. They also have their own art gallery.

CRAFTY BUSINESS

We've collected a wealth of resources to help get your crafty business going—everything from consigning and pricing to filing a DBA and writing a business plan—on our site, **www.pdxsupercrafty.com**.

INDEX

ABOUT THE AUTHORS

Susan Beal is a jewelry designer, editor, and freelance writer who divides her time between Portland and Los Angeles. She started her handmade business, susanstars, in 2000, and now sells her jewelry, lip balms, and handbags around the country and on her own website, **www.susanstars.com**. She writes about art, craft, and fashion for *BUST*, *ReadyMade*, *Venus*, and **www.getcrafty.com**. Susan also collaborates on independent films and performance art pieces with her husband, Andrew. She loves reading, secondhand shopping, and making new things.

Torie Nguyen suddenly decided one day that she would learn to sew for the sole purpose of creating fun, original handbags. Eleven months and many pinpricks and broken needles later, she launched her handbag line, Totinette (toe-tee-net), realizing a lifelong dream of owning her own business. Torie continues to expand her product line and now sells women's T-shirts, vintage jewelry, and small accessories on her website, **www.totinette.com**. Torie lives in Portland with her husband, Quentin, who is the man behind Monsieur T. T-shirts (**www.monsieurt. net**). She loves to craft, learn about art, read, knit scarves, make jewelry, garden, and cuddle with her dog, Annie.

Rachel O'Rourke received her master's degree in art therapy from the School of the Art Institute of Chicago. In 2000, she founded the Paper People Project (**www.paperpeopleproject.org**), an international arts installation against gun violence. She is also the design whiz behind Lucky Loo Loo Designs, jewelry inspired by the '40s, '50s, and '60s with a modern sculptural twist, while her hubby Danny is the sales, marketing, and website guru. Lucky Loo Loo was born in January 2003, after Danny bought Rachel a drill press for her birthday. Lucky Loo Loo Designs are sold across the United States, in Europe and Japan, and on their website, **www. luckylooloo.com**. When she is not designing jewelry, Rachel works as an art therapist and creates mixed media artwork.

Cathy Pitters is a mom, artist, and seamstress who lives in Portland, Oregon, with her husband, Greg, her son Levi, and two crazy cats. She spends most of her time in her flamingo-pink craft bunker, sewing for her business and building found object art. She sells her shrines and other goodies at art events around Portland as well as on her website, **www. bossanovababy.com**. After having her son in 1997, Cathy saw a lack of cool clothes for children and started Bossa Nova Baby, featuring funky clothing and accessories for kids as well as an assortment of other crafty oddities. In her spare time, Cathy volunteers at her son's school, digs for treasure at thrift stores, and drinks lots of coffee.

ABOUT THE ILLUSTRATOR AND PHOTOGRAPHERS

Ryan Berkley started drawing superheroes when he was three years old. As he grew up in Paradise, California, he developed his natural artistic talents with the encouragement of his lovely mother, Nancy. His grandfather is an accomplished artist and his younger brother Bo is also a gifted illustrator.

Comic books and movies have influenced his personal style, but he enjoys drawing a wide range of subjects. His illustrations have been used on brochures, T-shirts, posters, and murals.

He currently lives with his girlfriend Lucy in Portland, Oregon. See more of Ryan's work at **www.ryanberkley.com**.

Betsy Walton and **JD Hooge** run Morning Craft (**www.morningcraft.com**)—an online boutique featuring handmade goods and art—from their home in Portland, Oregon. Both are art school graduates hailing from the Midwest who migrated west to start their new lives amongst the rain-soaked Douglas firs.

Betsy is a painter and printmaker who has shown her work in solo and group shows in Milwaukee, Wisconsin, and Portland, Oregon. Her prints are included in *Ubersee 3,* a compendium of international art and design published by Die Gestalten Verlag. Betsy works at the Pacific Northwest College of Art and spends her spare time drawing, painting, and sewing.

JD is a designer, photographer, and programmer who spends most of his time staring into a sea of back-lit pixels. He works at a small interactive design studio in Portland by day and on a multitude of side projects by night. JD has contributed to several design/programming publications, served as part-time design faculty at the Milwaukee Institute of Art & Design, and was featured in *Print* magazine's 2005 New Visual Artists review.